M000192360

THE DIARY
OF A
VICTORIAN LADY

Emily Pountney ('Mama') with the twins Adelaide and Evelyn, 1841.

THE DIARY OF A VICTORIAN LADY

Scenes from her Daily Life 1864–1865

Illustrated by Adelaide Pountney

EXCELLENT PRESS
Ludlow

First published in 1998 by
Excellent Press
Palmers House
7 Corve Street
Ludlow, Shropshire SY8 1DB

ISBN 1 900318 05 9

Printed in Great Britain

Acknowledgements

The diaries of my great aunt Adelaide were discovered in the attic when I was moving house from Uley, Gloucestershire. I should like to thank Mr Duff Hart-Davis, my former neighbour, for introducing me to my publisher, and Mrs Glynis Taylor who transcribed the diaries. Grateful thanks also to Dr Jane Harris who enabled me to obtain expert advise from Miss Jane Bradish-Ellames. We were greatly assisted by Mrs Mary Mills from Wolverhampton Archives Department who discovered the date of Adelaide's birth and the birth dates of her siblings. The Rev John Hopcraft, Vicar of St John's, Wolverhampton, kindly assisted me with my enquiries and Mr Peter Hickman, the parish historian, was particularly helpful in discovering essential information about Adelaide's father. Special thanks are due to Mr David Blomfield for his skilful editing of the diaries. Most important of all, I am grateful to my sister Mrs Gillian Berkeley who has done almost all of the hard work involved in the research into Adelaide's life and times.

Rachel Sillett

FAMILY TREE

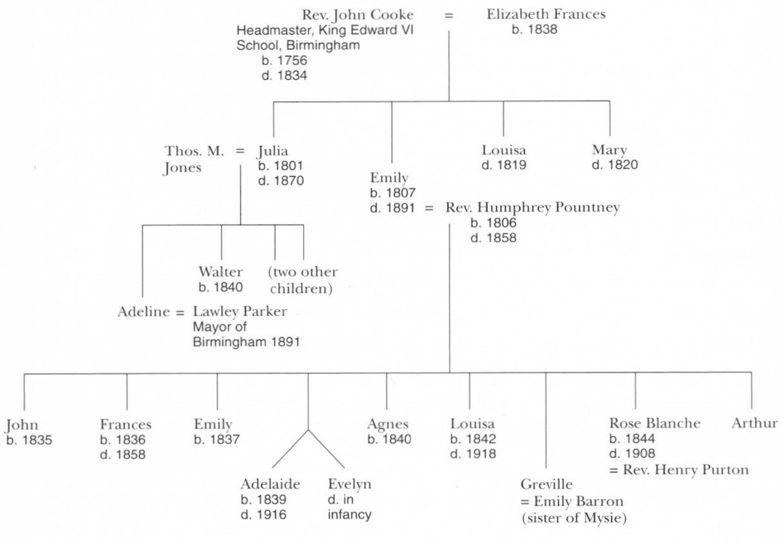
Rev. John Cooke
Headmaster, King Edward VI School, Birmingham
b. 1756
d. 1834
=
Elizabeth Frances
b. 1838
Thos. M. Jones
=
Julia
b. 1801
d. 1870
Emily
b. 1807
d. 1891
=
Rev. Humphrey Pountney
b. 1806
d. 1858
Louisa
d. 1819
Mary
d. 1820
Walter
b. 1840
(two other children)
Adeline = Lawley Parker
Mayor of Birmingham 1891
John
b. 1835
Frances
b. 1836
d. 1858
Emily
b. 1837
Agnes
b. 1840
Louisa
b. 1842
d. 1918
Rose Blanche
b. 1844
d. 1908
= Rev. Henry Purton
Arthur
Adelaide
b. 1839
d. 1916
Evelyn
d. in infancy
Greville
= Emily Barron
(sister of Mysie)

Adelaide and her Diary

Adelaide Pountney wrote and illustrated diaries for each of the years from 1863 to 1870. We know this because her diaries for these years were handed down to her niece and subsequently to her great niece. (She may have kept a diary in other years, but if so they have not survived.) Within those years she left many days blank, and in some years pages have been torn out of the diaries – by whom, and for what reason, we do not know. This edition includes only the years 1864 and 1865, the two years for which most entries survive.

In the diaries we meet Adelaide Pountney at the age of twenty-three, and the image she projects of herself is of an ordinary, very conventional, young lady of the Victorian leisured classes. Yet, there are several indications that Adelaide was in fact anything but ordinary. Not only are the diaries themselves a remarkable artistic achievement – thanks to Adelaide's gift for observation and her talent for drawing – but it seems that she may have deliberately omitted certain elements of her own story, leaving no more than the occasional hint of what might lie behind the gaps.

Certainly, from the little that is known of her family, it is clear that Adelaide's young life had been anything but conventional. In fact, her family had over the previous ten years endured a series of disasters.

To all appearances, the Pountneys were a typical well-to-do Victorian family. Adelaide's father was a Church of England clergyman, the Reverend Humphrey Pountney. Her mother was the daughter of another clergyman, the headmaster of the King Edward VI School, Birmingham. Adelaide had nine brothers and sisters – a not unusual number in those days. (See the family tree at the front).

Yet, if the Pountneys were apparently typical of their class, Humphrey Pountney himself was a far from typical clergyman. For twenty-six years he was vicar of St John's, Wolverhampton, a parish dependent, like many at the time, on the support of a middle class congregation. In the 1850s, there was a growing concern in Wolverhampton over the plight of local miners, who were being paid largely in vouchers that could be cashed only in specific local shops, which in turn could price their goods as high as they wished. In the parish of St John's, however, it was only the vicar, and not the congregation, who was concerned at this exploitation of the poor. When their vicar went so far as to give evidence to parliament against the mineowners, two-thirds of the St John's congregation decided to worship elsewhere.

When Humphrey was given sabbatical leave by his bishop in 1858, the Pountneys went to Munich. Exactly what happened there is not known, but the story has been handed down the generations that almost half the Pountney family, including Humphrey Pountney himself, fell victims to a typhoid epidemic. Certainly only five of the children survived to be mentioned in the diaries: Adelaide, Louisa, Greville, Rose and Arthur. Among those who died young was Adelaide's twin sister Evelyn.

The remaining Pountneys returned to Britain and settled in Leamington Spa. Despite the loss of so many of the family, including the breadwinner, they seem to have maintained their comfortable way of life without too much difficulty. They bought a large house, which they later let out, and moved from one to another of a series of rented properties in Devon. It seems that this move was prompted by the ill health of Arthur and Adelaide, one or both of whom apparently suffered from bronchial disorders.

By the time of the move to Devon, the family unit was contracting further. Greville had left to make a home in Australia where he would be joined in 1865 by his fiancée Emily Barron. (The Barron sisters were among Adelaide's closest friends in Leamington, and appear frequently in the diaries, under a bewildering variety of nicknames and alternative spellings: Emily/Emy, Mysie/Maria/Myria/Myriar, and Jane.) Meanwhile, Rose, the youngest Pountney, was being courted by a widower, the Reverend Henry Purton, whom she would marry in 1865, the ceremony charmingly illustrated in Adelaide's diary.

In the diaries, we see the Pountneys engaged in the customary social activities – shopping, soirées, churchgoing, teaching in the Sunday school, charity work. There are the endless rounds of 'visiting', when visitors would either have left their visiting cards or been offered tea and conversation. (See the Notes)

Despite Adelaide's occasional references to her having no money, it is clear that the family had no difficulties in keeping up with their neighbours. They might not keep a carriage of their own in Leamington – they lived so close to their friends and the shops that they had little need of one – but when they moved to the country they kept a horse and phaeton. It is not clear how many servants they employed – Adelaide seldom mentions them – but the houses they rented were substantial. The family clearly never cooked their own meals, and their domestic duties were restricted to a little light dusting, ordering meals, and handing out sheets and towels to the servants from the linen chest.

Although Adelaide was the oldest surviving child, it seems that initially she took on fewer responsibilities than her younger sisters. Louisa and Rose taught regularly at Sunday School and took care of the linen chest at home; Adelaide did so only when her sisters were away. Again it was Louisa, not Adelaide, who left home to look after the ailing Arthur. It may well have been that Adelaide was seen as semi-invalid. She makes very little of her colds, but it is clear that her mother was deeply concerned and ordered her to stay at home. If this was so, the move to the south coast was really effective, as Adelaide would not die until 1916, at Exeter. She was then aged seventy-four.

Sadly the move south was less effective for Arthur. We do not know when he died, but must assume it could have been as early as the closing months of 1865. Certainly he is never mentioned in the diaries from then on. This raises a point that has to intrigue any reader of the diaries. Why does Adelaide say nothing of it?

Clearly she was very fond of Arthur, as can see from her references to him throughout 1864/5. Did she feel unable to deal with painful matters in the diary? (Similarly Aunt Clifton – probably a great aunt on her mother's side – is described as very ill in June 1864, is visited urgently by relatives, and then is never mentioned again. One must assume she died, though the diary says nothing.) Could it be that such losses are marked by blank unillustrated pages or even that they were recorded and torn out later?

One other point must be made. In the diaries of these two years Adelaide says nothing of any romantic attachments of her own. She is equally private in the following years, though every now and then she gives a hint of her more intimate feelings, most notably with this entry on the first page of her diary for 1867: 'Cecil Lionel – si tu savais combien je t'aime.' Nowhere, of course, is there any indication of who the mysterious 'Cecil Lionel' might be. She never married.

All readers have the same opportunity to reach their own conclusions on this – and of course other matters too – and therein lies the magic of the diaries. They tell us directly so much about how people looked and how people lived. They are far more subtle about how people loved. That is left for us to read between the lines.

1. FRIDAY. Emily B. went with us to Church [illegible] [illegible]. I dined at the Barrons Called with Emy on Miss Blackwood, upon Mrs Chapman with Mamma Mr Purton dined with us First frost this winter

2. SATURDAY. Went to drawing class. Mr Purdon called in [illegible]. Cold. frosty weather

Mama LP (MrP) and NBP

3 SUNDAY. LES. M.—Isa. 41, Matt. 2. E.—Isa. 43, Rom. 2.
Went to Church twice Mr Purton & Emily came to supper

WB MrP. AMP EP RBP Mrs Pountney

4 MONDAY. Called with Mamma on the Carters Louisa & I went to a Soirée at Miss J Blackwoods

MrP MrB MrF

LP Mrs H. Miss C. EB. D C. Miss P, Mr L. WB. Miss L. AMP. Mrs F. Miss Beeton

5 TUESDAY. Walked out with Mysie. to Gleeclub with Mamma awfully cold

Dear Maria AMP.

6 WEDNESDAY. [Epiphany.] We all went to see the skating on the Leam Emily spent the evening here

MrsP. AMP.

Americans

The new walk
The Avon

4 THURSDAY. The Pinches, Leighs and Fry, Blackwood called. walked out with Maria. Mysie, & Emily stayed tea

scene, dear Maria knocking my hat about in the merest fun

5 FRIDAY. Jane and Miss Greenlaw called. I went out shopping alone.

6 SATURDAY. To drawing class. I spent the evening with Mysie Frost is come back

Mysie AMP.

7 SUNDAY. [Quinquagesima Sunday.]
LES.. *M.*—Gen. 9 to v. 20, Mark 7. *E.*—Gen. 12, 2 Cor. 3.

To school and church as usual cold !!!

AMP teaching

8 MONDAY. [Half-Quarter Day.]

Called with Mama upon Mrs Cobbe Louisa and I spent the evening at Miss Blackwoods. Rhodes, Greenlaw, Croker, Jane., Frost

9 TUESDAY. Frost [Shrove Tuesday.] Mr Graham is married

To clothing club district. To Mrs Percox with Rose. E and J. Barron, Miss Greenlaw and Miss Blackwood spent the evening here. Mrs Carter called

10 WEDNESDAY. Frost [Ash Wednesday.] To church, I called at the Barrons, Greek lesson, at which I, as usual, distinguished myself.

11 THURSDAY. Called with Mamma on Miss Harris and Gibbs Rose and Louisa went to a soirée at the Barrons. stayed all night

AMP Mamma
Playing at chess

12 FRIDAY. Went out alone to buy a fowl. Louisa and Rose came home. Barrons and Miss Greenlaw called Frost is gone !!!!!!! Mr Purton dined here

AMP MrsRous

13 SATURDAY. Stayed at home with a cold Miss Blackwood called so did E and J. Barron so did Mr Purton
Greek lesson

The lesson

E

14 SUNDAY. [Quadragesima Sunday.]
LES.. *M.*—Gen. 19 to v. 30. Mark 14. *E.*—Gen. 22, 2 Cor. 10.

Stayed at home with a bad cold

15 MONDAY. Dined at the Barrons walked afterwards with Mysie. Greek lesson

16 TUESDAY. To clothing club district. called on Miss about cards. showery weather. Mr Purton came in the evening.

17 WEDNESDAY. Rose went to stay with Mrs Warren. Mamma Louisa and I drank tea at Mrs Cobbes

18 THURSDAY. Mamma and I called with Miss Blackwood on Mrs Mcgregor.

Mrs P. Miss B. AMP. coming out of Miss B.s house

19 FRIDAY. Snowed continually the whole day. I went to see the Barrons walked out with Mysie. Miss Blackwd. called. Greek lesson.

The Barrons drawing room

EB AMP MB

20 SATURDAY. Went to drawing class. Rose and I went to see the Barrons

AMP Miss Burgess Hobson No.2. Hobson No.1 Miss Gubbins

21 SUNDAY. LES..*M.*—Gen. 27, Luke 4. *E.*—Gen. 34, Galat. 4.
To church twice; no school because of the snow

Snow!! 22 MONDAY. Went to read to Smith; to see A. Mucklow and Miss Baker. Walked out with Jane. Mr Purton came in the even Rose returned from Mrs Warrens

LP Mama AMP Supper

23 TUESDAY. Went club col spent the rest of the day at the Barrons

Mysie Emy Jane AMP

24 WEDNESDAY. Louisa and I went to Emscote church with Miss Baker. Walked after dinner with Jane. Emy and Mysie came to tea Arctic weather

LP AMP. Miss B

Mr Lewthwaite going to read

cold !!! FEBRUARY, 1864.

25 THURSDAY. Drew all day. Went out with Rose. Jane and Sophy Davies came to tea

26 FRIDAY. Went to post Greville's letters with ~~Mamma~~. Mamma Emy. Louisa and I went to church in evening.

27 SATURDAY. To drawing class. Mamma and I went to the church to choose a pew then to see A Mucklow and Mrs Cobbe Mr Purton dined here

3 Mrs Cuffs E 2

28 SUNDAY. LES. *M.*—Gen. 39, Luke 11. *E.*—Gen. 42, Eph. 5.
Too wet for school, to church twice

29 MONDAY. Rain all day Walked home with Mysie. Greek begun again & ended!

1 TUESDAY. Went to district. After dinner Mysie and I went to read to Mrs Neal. tea at the Barrons

2 WEDNESDAY. Louisa and Rose dined with Mrs Cobbe. Mamma and I went in the evening to Christ Church. Mr Purton came

3 THURSDAY. Went to Hordan to have a tooth stopped, well done took our club money to Miss Baker. Mamma and I with Mysie and Jane went to hear a concert by Mr Mann's class at Warwick Lobegesang of Mendlesohn's Mr Coleridge !!!!!!!!!!!!!!!

1 Miss M Corrie
2 Jane
3 ~~Mamma~~ Mysie
4 Mamma
5 Miss Corrie
6 AMP
Mr Coleridge singing

4 FRIDAY. Went into town with Mamma and Rose. Mr Reay and the Greenways called. Mrs Cobbe Mr Williams Jane & Mr. Purton dined with us.

5 SATURDAY. Went to drawing class. To Christ church with Mama Mr Purton dined with us.

6 SUNDAY. LES.. *M.*—Gen. 43. Luke 17. *E.*—Gen. 45, Col. 1.
Too wet for school, to church twice

7 MONDAY. Walked out with Mysie played duets together went to Christ church in evening made late by mad bulls. Mr Purton came to dinner

8 TUESDAY. Rain all day so could not collect for club. Went to Hordern to have old stopping taken out of tooth. Tea at Barrows

9 WEDNESDAY. Snow all day without cessation. Mr Purton dined here. Greek lesson.

10 THURSDAY. To Hordens with Jane. Miss Blackwood called To Christ Church with Mamma Mysie dined with us

11 FRIDAY. Drew all morning. Mrs Meredith called. Went with Mamma into Springfield street called on Mrs Cobbe

12 SATURDAY. Mr Williams called. Louisa and I called on the Mcgrigors and Leighs, not at home. Walked home with Miss Blackwood had a chat until church time

13 SUNDAY. LES..*M.*—Exo. 3, Luke 24. *E.*—Exo. 5, 1 Thes. 4.

To Church and school called with Mamma on Mrs Woodhouse

14 MONDAY, Called on the Greenways, Mr Purton walked with I came to stay with Miss Blackwood

15 TUESDAY, Went to clothing club Jane called. We went in the evening to Mrs Warrens. Frys and Leigh

16 WEDNESDAY.. Went to Church, called after on Mrs Wood house and on my family

17 THURSDAY. Mr and Willie Barron called Miss Blkwd
2 I walked on the Lillington road. Called on Mrs Warren
tea at the Barrons

18 FRIDAY. [Cam. Lent Term ends.] To Church, went
to see Myriar Lunched at home. went to hear
Mrs Dale play the organ Rose Mr Purton and
Jane spent the evening. Rose stayed all night

19 SATURDAY. [Oxford Lent Term ends.]
Walked out with Myriar Went home
lunched Miss Mc grigor Mc crae and Mysie
spent the evening

20 SUNDAY. LES. . *M.*—Exo. 9, Mat. 26. *E.*—Exo. 10, Heb. 5 to v. 11.
[Palm Sunday.] To Church three times
Took Miss Mcgrigor in the evening

21 MONDAY. To Church. called with Mamma on Mrs Woodhouse Miss Mcgrigor called. Miss Brenton Mysie and Louisa came to tea

22 TUESDAY. To club came home from Miss Blackwood's Walked to Lillington with Mamma Rose and Mr Burton to Christ Church

and Mamma

23 WEDNESDAY. To Church I called with Mamma on Miss Blackwood Louy Miss Aston and Jane & Mysie & I walked to Cubbington

24 Thursday. To Church morn and even Mama and I called on Mrs Bobbe Mr Purton and his brother came in the evening

25 Friday. [Lady Day. Good Friday.]

Les. M.—Genesis 22 to v. 20, John 18. E.—Isaiah 53, 1 Peter 2.

To Christ Church with Rose called on Barroness Blkwood went with Miss Aston and Gibby to hear W Purton play the organ in Parish Church The two Purtons came to tea

26 Saturday. I posted papers for Greville I called on Mr Bertlgote walked out with Jane Mr Purton dined with us

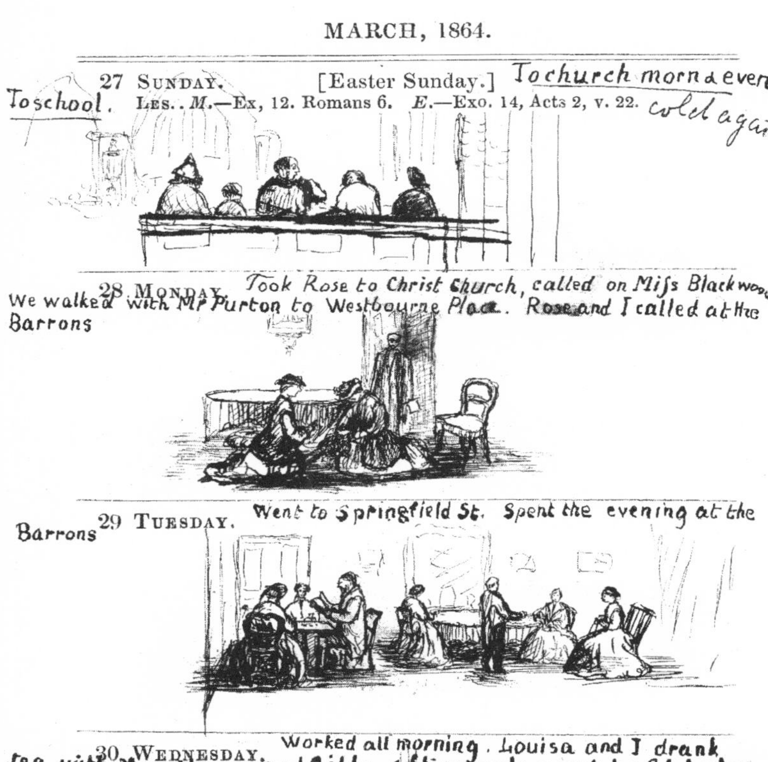

27 SUNDAY. [Easter Sunday.] To church morn & even

To school. LES.. *M.*—Ex, 12. Romans 6. *E.*—Exo. 14, Acts 2, v. 22. cold agai[n]

28 MONDAY. Took Rose to Christ Church, called on Miss Blackwoo[d]

We walked with Mr Purton to Westbourne Place. Rose and I called at the Barrons

29 TUESDAY. Went to Springfield St. Spent the evening at the Barrons

30 WEDNESDAY. Worked all morning. Louisa and I drank tea with Miss Harris and Gibbs, afterwards went to St Lukes

LP

Miss Harris Miss Gibbs AMP

31 THURSDAY. Mamma and I called on Mrs Dawes

Lucy Dawes AMP mamma

1 FRIDAY. [Cam. Easter Term begins.]

Louisa and I called at the Barrons. they all with Mrs Bernside came to tea

2 SATURDAY. I called a.m. on Miss Bla[illegible]d Mamma and I went out shopping after luncheon and to Christ church. Mrs Fry called to wish us goodbye

Mrs Fry Mamma AMP

3 SUNDAY. LES.. *M.*—Num. 16, John 21. *E.*—Num. 22, Heb. 5.
[Low Sunday.] To church morning and afternoon. Mama and I called to see Miss Blackwood

4 MONDAY. I called on Mrs H Davies Mamma Louisa and I went to the station to meet Aunt Clifton who didnot come. Miss Leigh called

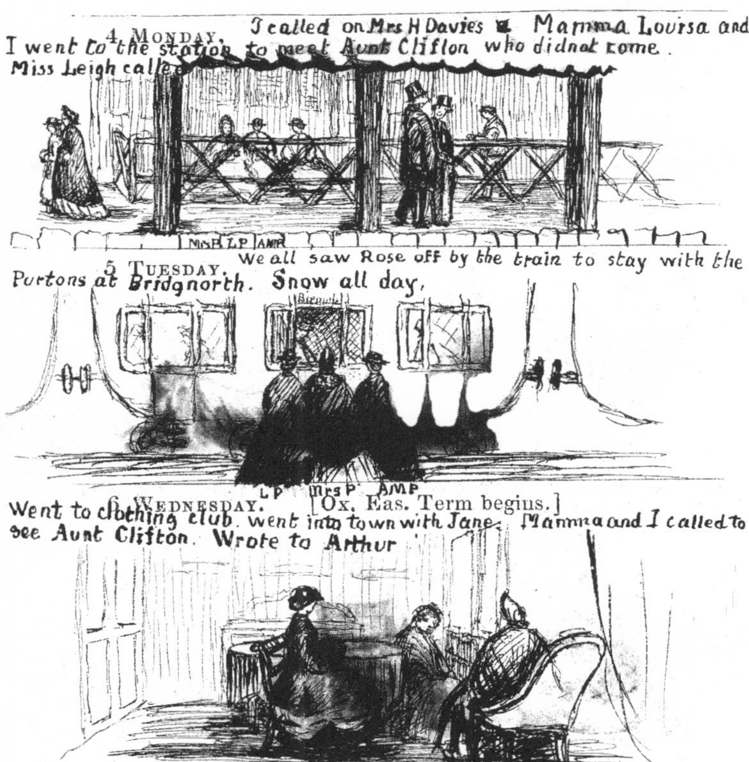

5 TUESDAY. We all saw Rose off by the train to stay with the Purtons at Bridgnorth. Snow all day.

6 WEDNESDAY. [Ox. Eas. Term begins.] Went to clothing club. went into town with Jane. Mamma and I called to see Aunt Clifton. Wrote to Arthur

7 THURSDAY. Emily Barron called. I called on Miss Blackwood
Aunt Clifton dined with us

AMP Miss Blackwood.

8 FRIDAY. [Fire Insurance ceases.]
went with Mamma to Springfield St. I called to see Aunt Clifton, coffee at the Barrons.

MB AMP EB Aunt Cliftons lodgings

9 SATURDAY. Walked after dinner with Jane we went to Christch
Emily and Mysie came in the evening

AMP Jane Barron and friends

10 SUNDAY. LES.. *M.*—Num. 23, 24, Acts 7. *E.*—Num. 25, Heb. 12.
To school and church, to Trinity church in the evening we went to see Aunt Clifton after dinner. letter from Rose

11 MONDAY. I went to the postoffice for Aunt Clifton, called on the Barrons.. Walked after dinner with Mysie. to Christ church, even.

AMP MEB

12 TUESDAY. Miss Blackwood called Emily Barron stayed tea

EB mama LP AMP

13 WEDNESDAY. Alfred called. Mama and I went out called on Aunt Clifton Mrs Dawes and Lucy called. I had a letter from Greville. wrote to Arthur.

14 THURSDAY. Lovy's birthday. I gave her nothing as I have no money Jane and the Craigs called. Mamma Louisa and I went to see Aunt Clifton and afterwards to buy muslin curtains

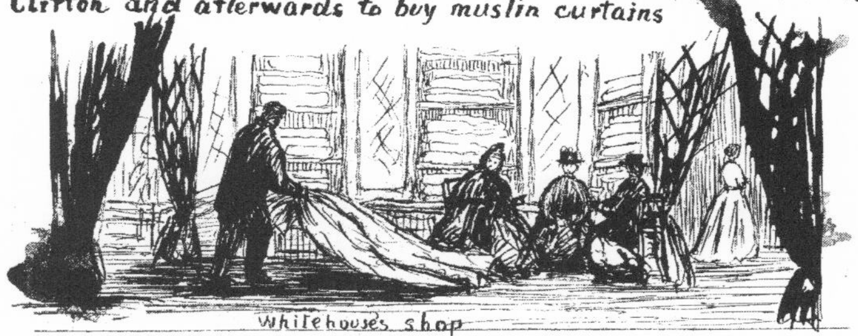

Whitehouse's shop

15 FRIDAY. Went to [Easter Term begins.] Springfield district, Called at the Barrons. Mamma Louisa and I drank tea with Aunt Clifton.

Aunt C Mamma L and AMP playing at casino

16 SATURDAY. We dusted the books in the den. Emily Barron called

LP Mamma AMP

17 SUNDAY. LES. *M.*—Deut. 4, Acts 14. *E.*—Deut. 5, 1 Pet. 1.

Went to school to church morn and even Mamma and I went to see Aunt Clifton

18 MONDAY. Mrs Banbury & friend called. Sat in the garden some time with Mamma Jane came to tea

19 TUESDAY. To district. Walked out with Mysie tea at the Barrons. I called on the Pinches

20 WEDNESDAY. Walked out with Jane. Went to Springt with Mamma to Christ Church after. Miss Blhndcame

21 THURSDAY. Came to stay with Jane Barron during the absence of dear Maria & Emy Lister. Went with me to choose trimming for my bonnet. Jane & I walked in garden after Coffee. Miss B came in the evening

22 FRIDAY. Walked out shopping with Myssie who returned from Warwick with Emy early. I came home. Went out after dinner and to Christ Ch with M. and L.

EB Myriar

AMP

23 SATURDAY. Went out early to buy ribbon for bonnet which Miss Birch and I trimmed at once. The Temples called. I took Jane to call on Aunt Clifton thence to shew Jane the door of the national schools. I went afterwards to Springfield St

24 Sunday. Les. *M.*—Deut. 6, Acts 21. *E.*—Deut. 7, 2 Pet, 3.
To Church and school twice Jane took a class called to see Mrs Meredith thence to Aunt Clifton Mr Purton came to supper

25 Monday. Walked in the gardens with Mysie after dinner read aloud. tea at the Barrons

26 Tuesday. To my district Went with Mysie to see Aunt Clifton Mysie took her flowers, I went to Christ Church Wrote to Greville

27 Wednesday. Miss Blkwood and Mrs Cobbe called. Lucy and I went to Cuttings to get a sash for my hair brought mamma to church from Aunt Cliftons

28 Thursday. Louisa and I called at the Barrons (not at home) bought a silk umbrella (a present from Mamma) To Christ Church. Into gardens afterwards with M and L Mrs Carter called

29 Friday. Went to see Mrs Riffs came home by Barrons Emily gave me some port wine, lunched with Miss Blackwood. Called with Mamma on Mrs Meredith and Mrs Tarratt. tea at the Barrons

30 Saturday. Went again to drawing class which is now in a palatial apartment in the Public Hall Windsor street Mamma and I called on the Temples Mcgregor and Belchers To Christ Chur

MAY, 1864.

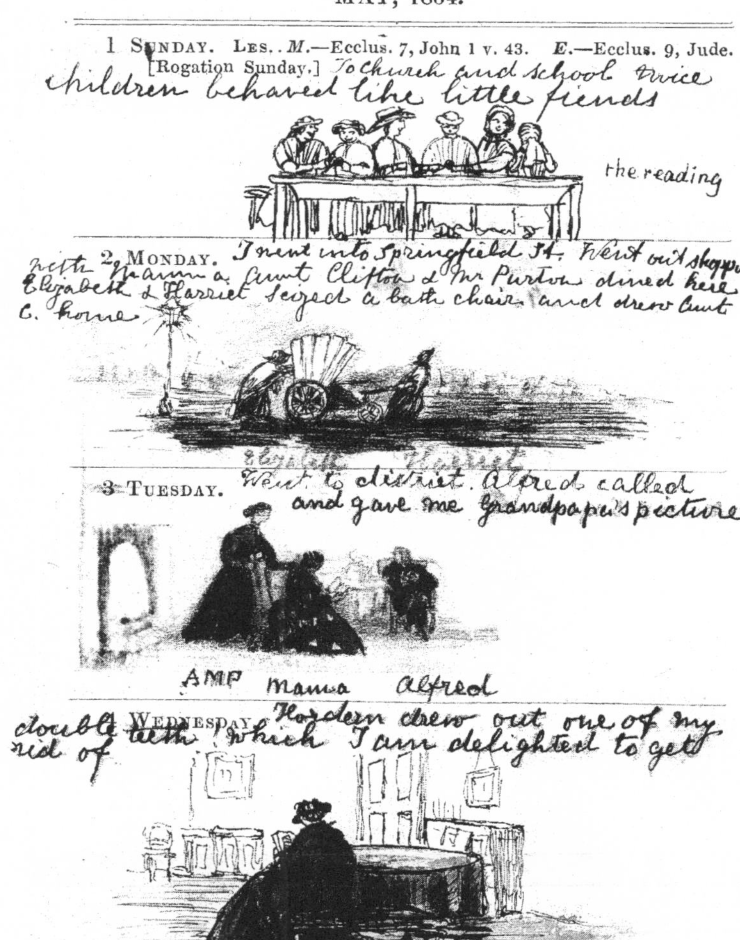

1 SUNDAY. LES. *M.*—Ecclus. 7, John 1 v. 43. *E.*—Ecclus. 9, Jude.
[Rogation Sunday.] To church and school twice children behaved like little fiends

2 MONDAY. I went into Springfield St. Went out shopping with Mamma a Aunt Clifton & Mr Purton dined here Elizabeth & Harriet seized a bath chair and drew Aunt C. home

3 TUESDAY. Went to district. Alfred called and gave me Grandpapa's picture

4 WEDNESDAY. Hordern drew out one of my double teeth which I am delighted to get rid of

Horderns drawingroom
AMP waiting until her turn comes to have her tooth dra

5 THURSDAY. [Ascension. Holy Thursday.]

At home all day drew morn. and afternoon Jane called Emy & Myriar came to tea I wrote to Arthur

6 FRIDAY. Louisa and I took the club money to Miss Baker into town shopping and to Christ Church with Mamma

7 SATURDAY. Went to drawing class. two new pupils. Myriar called

8 SUNDAY. LES. . *M.*—Deut. 12, Matt. 6. *E.*—Deut. 13, Romans 7.
[Half-Quarter Day.] Went to Church in the afternoon

9 MONDAY. Miss Blackwood called [Easter Term ends.] Mamma Louisa & I went out shopping I went to see Aunt Clifton. Louisa ordered a boot at Rishes with a very deep military heel

10 TUESDAY. Went to district. Emily called. Mamma Louisa and I went out shopping I bought a hat with a broad brim in spite of Louisa

Scene Perry's shop
LP. advising AMP to adopt the very becoming hat without any brim at all
AMP decides this time upon following her own instinct which tells her not to choose LP's favourite shape

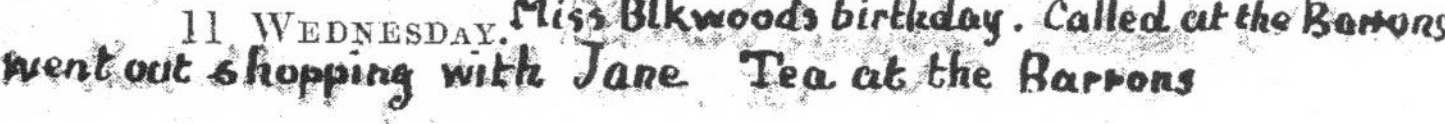

11 WEDNESDAY. Miss Blkwoods birthday. Called at the Barrons went out shopping with Jane Tea at the Barrons

The Mariner is probably coming home on Saturday

MAY, 1864.

12 THURSDAY. Drew all morning went out shopping after dinner with M. and L. J. B. Miss Blkwd & Baines came to tea Mrs Belcher called

13 FRIDAY. Mamma, Louisa & I sat in the gardens after dinner Rose and I went to a soirée at the Carters.

14 SATURDAY. [Ox. Eas. Term ends.] Went to drawing class To church in the evening with Mamma called at Miss Blackwoods Arthur came home and brought somebody with him

MAY, 1864.

children want Rose back again

15 SUNDAY. [Whit Sunday.]

LES., *M.*—Deut. 16 to v. 18, Acts 10 to v. 34. *E.*—Isaiah 11, Acts 19 to v. 21.

went to Church and school, walked afternoon service with Emily in the fields

16 MONDAY. Rose I and Toby went into the town Into the gardens afterwards with Mamma town crowded

17 TUESDAY. To district Went into gardens with Arthur and Toby Tea at the Barrows

18 WEDNESDAY. [Ox. Trin. Term begins.]

I and Arthur called upon Mrs Cobbe and the Pinchess. I had tea at Miss Blackwoods we all viz: Emy, Jane, Myriar, Blkwood, Toby & AMP walked in the fields after sunset

19 THURSDAY. Louisa and I went to meet Mrs Bolton at the station thunder and lightning prevented our going out again.

20 FRIDAY. Mama and I took Mrs Bolton to the station a.m and are now sitting under a tree in the gardens with the sun blazing around! I called on Miss Blkm Another thunderstorm. Miss Dawes called

21 SATURDAY. Jane Miss Burnside Miss Rhodes and I went by the omnibus to Warwick to see the castle

22 SUNDAY. [Trinity Sunday. Trin. Term begins.]

LES. M.—Genesis 1, Matthew 3. E.—Genesis 18, 1 John 5.

To school once, children more tractable but still want Rose back, To church morn and afternoon walked in fields with dear Myriar sat on an agricultural implement

23 MONDAY. Mysie and I went to see Mrs Neal then back to tea with the Barrons stayed all night because my family never sent for me

24 TUESDAY. [Q. Victoria b., 1819.] Came home. To distr with Toby. Called wiht Mamma on Aunt Clifton, to gardens afterwards Dear Myriar dined with us.

25 WEDNESDAY. Mama Emily & I called on the Wyers afterwards sat in the gardens joined by Jane

(Syers family playing croquet) Jane AMP

26 THURSDAY. Mr Male called. The mariner I and Toby went to buy a cream cheese for dinner. Aunt Clifton dined here

27 FRIDAY. Mamma and I went into Springfield St. home through gardens

28 SATURDAY. To drawing class. Louisa and I went out shopping, I bought a dress, home through gardens with family & Barrons Toby and Ossian were washed

29 SUNDAY. LES.. *M.*—Joshua 10, Mat. 27 *E.*—Joshua 23, 1 Cor. 12.

To skhool once To Church morn and afternoon. children better with the exception of Elisa Mucklow.

my class

30 MONDAY. Went out shopping with Louisa Lunched at the Barrons Miss Bernside came to wish us goodbye. Myria read, at least tried to read to me

In the Den

31 TUESDAY. Rain all day so did no collecting. Mama and I went out called at Aunt Cliftons, did much work.

our garden door

1 WEDNESDAY. Went with T to my district. Mamma and I called on the Bakers and Carters. Sat in the gardens with Myria and Jane

2 THURSDAY. Drew the monk all morn. Louisa & I went out, home through the gardens Tea at the Barrons

3 FRIDAY. Drew all morning. Mariner and I walked to Radford mama and I went to see Aunt Clifton after dinner.

4 SATURDAY. Went to drawing class Mama and I went into the gardens E and M Barron and Miss Blackwood joined us.

5 SUNDAY. LES.. *M.*—Judges 4, Mark 6. *E.*—Judges 5, 2 Cor. 3.

Mama Emily and I went to Whitnash church morn. To parish church evening

6 MONDAY. The Warners and Mrs Cobbe called Emily dined with us

7 TUESDAY. Went to district. To the Gar[illegible] with Mama First day of the militia band

8 WEDNESDAY. Drew all morning. Mamma Louisa and I called upon Mrs Warner

9 THURSDAY. I dined at the Barrons read Nicholas Nickleby to Mysie brought her (Myriar) back to tea. Louisa and I went to play casino with Aunt Clifton.

10 FRIDAY. Louisa and I dined with Mrs Cobbe, and afterwards we all, including Mrs Warner and Sarah drove to Kenilworth. Tea at the Hotel. Mamma and I went to see Aunt Clifton after tea

11 SATURDAY. Mysie and I went to see Mrs Neal. Arthur and Rose went to Yardley Wood. Louisa and I tore about in the rain all day brought Sarah Warner home to dine with us. I went to see Aunt Clifton after dinner

12 SUNDAY. LES. *M.*—1 Sam. 2, Mark 12. *E.*—1 Sam 3, 2 Cor. 9.
To church in the morning. Mamma and I went to see Aunt Clifton who is very ill

13 MONDAY. [Trinity Term ends.]
I bottled 9 qts gooseberries and made jam of some more.

14 TUESDAY. Emily Gilpin came

15 WEDNESDAY. Aunt Julia came Miss Blackwood called

16 Thursday.

17 Friday. William Clifton came in the evening

18 Saturday

19 SUNDAY. LES.. *M.*—1 Sam. 12, Luke 3. *E.*—1 Sam. 13, Gal. 3.
Emily Barron and I went to Lillington church. am. Rose and I went to Parish church in the eveving
20 MONDAY. [Accession Queen Victoria.]
Mrs Cobbe &
Miss Blkwd calla
Mysie and I went into the fields and read aloud.
MR AMP.
21 TUESDAY. [Proclamation Queen Victoria.]
Toby and I went to my district
22 WEDNESDAY. Jane and I walked out after dinner, sat in the gardens
Jane AMP Miss Blk

23 THURSDAY. Jane and I went to the Guy's cliff fields with the little sums The Bakers called for the club money

24 FRIDAY. [Midsum. Day. Cam. Eas. Term ends.]
Rose and I went out together (first time for months!!!) Kate Mackie came to tea

25 SATURDAY. Lucy Dawes called the Barrons and Miss Blkwood called Emily & Jane gave me a garnet brooch, & dear Myriar a pair of earrings to match!!! Miss Blkwood gave me a flower vase. Toby Carter came to see us.

26 SUNDAY. LES. *M.*—1 Sam. 15, Luke 9. *E.*—1 Sam. 17, Eph. 3.
Went to Parish Church morn and afternoon

27 MONDAY. Mama and I went out shopping. Miss Harris Jane, Mr and Mrs Haddon and Rebekah with Mrs Smith—Tibbitts called W. Barron dined with us.

28 TUESDAY. [Queen Victoria crowned, 1838.]
Arthur went back to Devonport, took Toby with him. I went out shopping alone and miserable in the rain with each hand full

29 WEDNESDAY. I went to my district. The Dawes's called to wish us goodbye. E. and M. Barron came

30 THURSDAY. Drew all morning. Louisa and I took a hospital ticket to Mrs Overton's doughter – Mad Cow in a garden!!! Louisa and I had tea at the Barrons. Mr & Mrs Ness & Miss Baker.

Muggins

1 FRIDAY. Mama and I called on the Corbetts, Temples, and Rebekah. Miss Blackwood came to tea

Mama Mrs Corbett

2 SATURDAY. Went to drawing class. W. Purton and young friend called. Alfred Clifton lunched with us. Mama Rose and I went to the gardens. the band is quite deafening

3 SUNDAY. LES.. *M.*—2 Sam 12, Luke 15. *E.*—2 Sam. 19, Phil. 3.

To school and church once.

4 MONDAY. The Farmers and Mr Reay called Emily and Mysie came to tea

5 TUESDAY. I went to see the Barrons. Mama and I called on the Haddons thence to the gardens. Fanny Fowke, Jane and W. Barron came to tea.

6 WEDNESDAY. Went to my district. Rose went with me to wish Mrs Warren The Barrons and Miss Blackwood farewell

7 THURSDAY. Rose went to stay at Llandudno with the Purtons. Mama took her to Birmingham. Louisa and I called at the Barrons & I bought for Louisa's Jam some glass Jars, being very superior to the china ones. and only /3 dearer the dozen.

8 FRIDAY. [Fire Insurance ceases.]
~~I~~ I dined and spent the evening at the Barrons. Went on the Avon sketching with Mysie and W. Barron

9 SATURDAY. [Ox. Trin. Term ends.]
Went to my drawing class for the last time. Mama I and Louisa went to hear the band play in the gardens.

10 SUNDAY. LES.. *M.*—2 Sam. 21, Luke 22. *E.*—2 Sam. 24, 1 Thes. 2
Went to school once, to church morn and even.

11 MONDAY. Jane called. I went out shopping alone. Mama Louisa and I drove to Sherbourne saw the New church

12 TUESDAY. Mama and I went into the gardens pleasanter than the last time.

13 WEDNESDAY. Went to my district. Mysie, W. Barron & I went sketching by the river Leam Mama J. & Emy Barron & Louy joined us I had tea at the Barrons

14 THURSDAY. Emily Barron dined with us. Miss Corrie spent the afternoon with us took her to hear the band play Louisa and I walked with her to the station

15 FRIDAY. [St. Swithin.] Mama, I, Jane and Mysie went into the gardens I wrote to Rose

selfish man to the left.

Mama Jane AMP Dear Maria by the river

16 SATURDAY. I dined at the Barrons Emy and went after dinner into the Newbold fields

17 SUNDAY. LES. *M.*—1 Kings 13, John 5. *E.*—1 Kings 17, 1 Tim. 1.
To school once, to church morning and even letter from Adeline inviting me to stay with them

18 MONDAY. Miss Blackwood called to say goodbye Mama Louisa and I went into the town shopping We drank tea at Mrs Warrens

19 TUESDAY. To district. I, Mysie and W. Barron went to play croquet at the Bakers. stayed tea at the Barrons

20 WEDNESDAY. Louisa and I called on the Hardwickes Jane and Mysie Barron came to tea

21 THURSDAY. I came to stay with the Lawley Parkers at Edgbaston

*self and railway companions

22 FRIDAY. Adeline and I came to stay at Yardley Wood School fête rain almost all day plenty of people in spite of it

23 SATURDAY. Down at eleven AMP. Adeline and I called upon the Miss Andertons and Mrs Parker stayed tea at the latter and walked back to Yardley Wood in the cool of the evening with Mr. L. Parker. Alfred dined at Mosely

24 SUNDAY. LES.. *M.*—1 Kings 18, John 12. *E.*—1 Kings 19, 2 Tim. 3.

To Church morn and even. We all vis Alfred Lawley and Adeline & AMP walked in fields after each service

25 MONDAY. We Returned to Edgbaston and went at once to the bazaar at Sutton Coldfield to assist at Mrs A Smiths stall

26 TUESDAY. Went again to Sutton Coldfield bazaar fine day Lawley came to fetch us home we walked in the park afterwards

27 WEDNESDAY. Stayed at home all day to rest ourselves

28 THURSDAY. Stayed at home all day Alfred came to dinner I wrote to Mama & Myria

AMP Aunt Julia Lawley Adeline

29 FRIDAY. Stayed at home all day

Adeline Playin AMP

30 SATURDAY. Adeline and I walked into Birmingham. got some duetts to play together.

AMP Adeline overture to Sampa

31 SUNDAY. LES. *M.*—1 Kings 21, John 19 *E.*—1 Kings 22, Heb. 3.
Adeline Lawley & I went to St Pauls church morn. We walked round by Old Edgbaston church after tea

1 MONDAY. [Lammas Day.] Wrote to Mama & Arthur.
Adeline and I went by train after dinner to Gravely Hill to call upon Mrs Smallwood

Adelme AMP M B.
Lawley St Station
after all that has transpired

2 TUESDAY. Miss C. Phipson spent the day here Adeline and I walked with her to the station.

3 WEDNESDAY. Letter from Mysie. at home all day

4 THURSDAY. Adeline and I walked into Birmingham brought back Blanche Taylor. Alfred and Emily Gilpin came to tea John Taylor came to supper.

Blanche T. Alfred, Adeline, J Taylor, Emily, Lawly, AMP

5 FRIDAY Alfred called Mrs Dalton called Adeline and I called to see Mrs Bents garden after tea Lawley Adeline and I walked to the reservoir. Walter Jones came to supper.

AMP Lawley Adeline

6 SATURDAY. Returned to Leamington Adeline & Walter Jones saw me depart by the train

7 SUNDAY. LES.. *M.*—2 Kings 5, Acts 5. *E.*—2 Kings 9, Heb. 10.
To church once, bad cold and hoarseness

8 MONDAY, Still very hoarse. The Miss Ainsworths called
Myria did not call Louisa had tea at the Barrons

9 TUESDAY. Cold is better I wrote to Adeline and Miss
Blackwood Emily and Mysie called.

10 WEDNESDAY. At home still all day. wrote to Arthur.
Mrs Cobbe called

11 THURSDAY. [Half-Quarter Day.]

Mama and I went into town. called on Mrs Tarratt. Mrs Warren called. The Barrons and their friends Miss Andrews & Hesse came to tea

12 FRIDAY. Emy I dined Mr with the Barrons, went after dinner with them to play croquet at the Bakers

13 SATURDAY. Jane came to see us in the morning. Mamma and I went out shopping after dinner into the gardens to hear the band

14 SUNDAY. LES.. *M.*—2 Kings 10, Acts 12. *E.*—2 Kings 18, Jam. 4.
Stayed at home all day because of my cough and hoarseness

15 MONDAY. Letters from Greville, Mrs Cobbe came to tea

16 TUESDAY. Louisa and I went out shopping a.m. Emily Barron came in the afternoon.

17 WEDNESDAY. Louisa went to stay with the Mackies at Coton on our way from the station we joined the Barrons in the Pump gardens played with them at croquet. I had a letter from Adeline.

18 THURSDAY. Willie Barron, Mrs Tarratt, & Mrs Cobbe called. Mama and I went out after dinner heard half an hour of the band in the gardens.

AMP — Mamma

19 FRIDAY. Emily Barron called, Mama and I went into town and gardens. Wrote to Greville and Rose. I won two games at chess of Ma[mma] !!!!!!!!!

Checkmate

20 SATURDAY. Mysie and I went to see Mrs Neal, played afterwards at croquet with the Barrons, drank tea with them. Emily stayed with Mamma

Jane, Miss Hess, Miss Andrews, AMP. | The Miss Smiths, W. & M. Barron

21 SUNDAY. LES.. *M.*—2 Kings 19, Acts 19. *E.*—2 Kings 23, 2 Pet. 1.

To Parish Church am. To Christ Church p.m, to try a pew. had a fire for the first time

22 MONDAY. I went to buy tickets for concert in the gardens. a.m. Mamma and I went out shopping after dinner.

Holly walk

23 TUESDAY. Went again to district. Emyly called. Mama and I went out after dinner

24 WEDNESDAY. Went out early to buy Jam pots I made 12 pots of most delicious plum Jam. 9 lbs. fruit & 6 3/4 lbs. sugar. Jane called I called upon Mrs Warren

25 THURSDAY. I called at the Barrons, found Emily washing at Miss Blackwoods house under Janes directions I careered about for lace etc to send Louisa

Scene
Miss Blkwds scullery

26 FRIDAY. I went out early shopping. Emy spent the day with us Mama Emy and I went out after dinner Greville's birthday

27 SATURDAY. Stayed at home Mrs Willmore and Jane called

28 SUNDAY. LES. *M.*—Jer. 5, Acts 26. *E.*—Jer. 22, 1 John 5.
To Christ church afternoon, too wet for morning church.

Going to our new pew in the gallery
Pew opener
AMP
Mamma

29 MONDAY. fine day W Barron called upon business matters
Mamma and I went into gardens and to Beck's library Jane joined us. The Barrons & friends called

Churchwardens family
Mama AMP Jane

30 TUESDAY. To club, I called at the Barrons. Mama and I went to the gardens. the band will not play again. Mrs Warren joined us.

Maria AMP Maria's room.

31 WEDNESDAY. Mama and I went to Christ Ch. I dined at the Barrons, played at croquet after dinner. Mama & I drank tea with Mrs Warren.

1 THURSDAY. Mama Jane Barron Miss Hesse and I went this afternoon to Stratford. Saw Shakspears house, the church then had tea at Shakspears inn home by the 7,10 train

2 FRIDAY. Jane Barron Miss Hesse and I went to the nationals shools feast. Kate Mackie and cousin called

3 SATURDAY. Mamma and I went out shopping in the morning

4 SUNDAY. LES.. *M.*—Jer. 35, Mat. 5. *E.*—Jer. 36, Rom. 5.
To school, and church morn. and afternoon tried another pew down stairs

5 MONDAY. Willie, Jane Barron and Miss Hesse called. Mama and I drove to Warwick home through Whitnash chose a drawing at Drure's to copy

6 TUESDAY. Wet morning Willie Barron came for letters to Clynn Mamma and I went into town sat in the gardens

7 WEDNESDAY. To clothing club. The Miss Anderton's, Jane and Miss Hesse called. I went after dinner to the butchers

8 THURSDAY. Mama and I called on Mrs Darwall Louy came home from Eton I dined at the Barrons

9 FRIDAY. Jane and Miss Hesse called. We went into the town, home through the gardens

Adderly's shop
Adderly showing Mama Louisa and AMP some clocks.

10 SATURDAY. Louisa and I went to fetch Mrs Washbrook. I had my hair cut by Frith morn. P.M. Mama and I called on the Miss Andertons and the H. Davie's's

Frith AMP L.P.

11 SUNDAY. LES.. *M.*—Ezekiel 2, Mat. 12. *E.*—Ezekiel 13, Rom. 12.
Went to school once to church morn and afternoon

12 MONDAY. The Miss Greenways & Mrs & Miss Darwall called
Jane and I walked to the mountain for fresh air. Lovely evening

13 TUESDAY. Jane and I walked to Warwick after dinner

14 WEDNESDAY. I went to district. Jane called and was weather bound until after dinner (For illustration see Saturday)

15 THURSDAY. (Jane called, Louisa and I called on the Miss Andertons
[illegible] I made 13 and a half pots of damson jam

(buying pears) [illegible] shop Mrs Rathbone

16 FRIDAY. Willie Barron called. I called on Miss Harris & Miss Gibbs
after dinner. Louisa dined at the Barrons

Miss Gibbs AMP

17 SATURDAY.

Louisa Mama Jane Barron AMP

Saturday I went to Becks, morning Mama and I walked to Whitnash p.m caught in a heavy rain sheltered at Mrs Cobbes

for illustration see Wednesday

Wednesday the picture belongs to Wodenstag

18 SUNDAY. LES.. *M.*—Ezekiel 14, Mat. 19. *E.*—Ezekiel 18, 1 Cor. 3.
To school once to church morn and afternoon

19 MONDAY. Called at the Barrons. AM. Walked to Whitnash round by the Tachbrook road with Jane, Miss Andrewes & W Barron.

20 TUESDAY. To district. drew all afternoon. Jane & Miss Andrewes came to tea

21 WEDNESDAY. Mama and I went to church walked afterwards past Lillington, home by Kenilworth road. Mr and Mrs H. Davies called

SEPTEMBER, 1864.

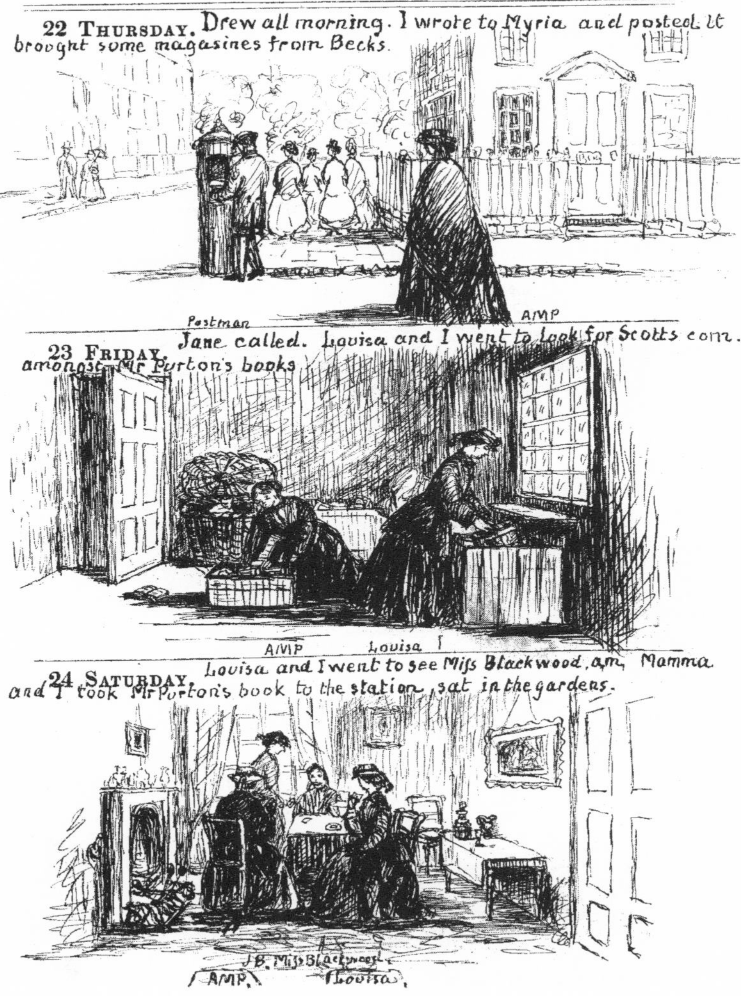

25 SUNDAY. LES. *M.*—Ezekiel 20, Matt. 26. *E.*—Ezekiel 24, 1 Cor. 10.
To school once, to church morn & afternoon

26 MONDAY. (Louisa and I called on Jane. I walked out with Miss Blackwood

27 TUESDAY. At home all day wrote to Adeline

(in front of our house) AMP waiting for Mama & Louisa's return to dinner

28. WEDNESDAY. Miss Blackwood called. Louisa and I went out after dinner sat in the gardens

LP AMP Churchwardens family | Paleman & friends

29 THURSDAY. [Michaelmas Day.]
Went to my district. I walked to Lillington with Jane and Miss Andrewes

30 FRIDAY. Louisa and I went to see Miss Blackwood and the Barrons
L. bought some epaulettes for her dress. Letter from Rose

1 SATURDAY. [Cam. Mich. Term begins.]
Louisa and I went to see Emy & Mysie Barron. Miss Blackwood and ~~M~~ Emily dined with us

OCTOBER, 1864.

2 SUNDAY. LES.. *M.*—Daniel 3, Mark 5. *E.*—Daniel 6, 2 Cor. 1.
Went to school, and church twice

3 MONDAY. Mamma Louisa and I went into town with Emily and Jane. Rose and Mr Purton came from Bridgnorth

4 TUESDAY. I went to my district. Rose and I went into town called to see the Barrons

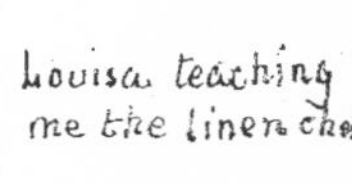

Louisa teaching me the linen chest

Louisa AMP

5 WEDNESDAY. Jane called. Louisa and I went to Springfield street and to Mrs Warrens and the Barrons, for L. to wish goodbye

AMP MrsArcher Louisa

6 THURSDAY. Dear old Louy went to Torquay to spend the winter with Arthur. We are all left very sad. I finished my drawing. Rose and I took Reinhardts Terence and other books to Mr Purton's old lodgings. bought a gold pen, a present from Mr Purton.

7 FRIDAY. Miss Blackwood came to breakfast & to see Mr Purton. Mr P. went away this morning. Mamma Rose & I went into town am, took my drawing to be framed. Rose and I went after dinner called on Mrs Warren. Jane called.

8 SATURDAY. Emily & Mysie Miss Harris and Gibbes called. I wrote to Louisa and counted out the linen stayed at home all day!!

9 SUNDAY. LES.. *M.*—Joel 2, Mark 12. *E.*—Micah 6, 2 Cor. 8.
To school once. took Louisa's class; to church twice

10 MONDAY. [Ox. Mich. Term begins.] Called on Mysie
Mama and I went to Warwick by omnibus. I spent the evening at Miss Blackwood

11 TUESDAY. Mysie and I went to see Mrs Neal dined with Myria and read Mosarts life to her.

12 WEDNESDAY. [Fire Insurance ceases.] Went to my district
I dined at the Barrons.

13 THURSDAY. The Miss Pinches called. Mamma and I called on the Ainsworths and Mrs Tarratt — letter from Loby

14 FRIDAY. Mrs Warren Mrs Staunton, Miss Blackwood, and Jane called Mamma and I went into the town called at Meres's.

Scene Meres's office

"Do you think I shall let my house Mr Meres?" "I do indeed mam there's a lady who wants the very thing furnished and a gentleman who would I believe take it unfurnished"

15 SATURDAY. Emily & Jane Barron & Miss Temple called. I walked with Jane to Whitnash after dinner.

AMR Jane

Whitnash bridge

16 SUNDAY. LES.. *M.*—Habak. 2, Luke 2. *E.*—Proverbs 1, Gal. 2.
To school and church twice (children less formidable)

17 MONDAY. Wrote to invite Kate Walker to stay with us
Rose and I were mde members of the free library by Mr H Davis

18. TUESDAY. Went to my district. Walked with Jane on Warwick road dined at the Barrons (Mrs Tarratt & Mrs Williams called)

19 WEDNESDAY. Mama [illegible]ss Blackwood and walked out this morn. towards Stoneleigh. Emily and Jane called

20 THURSDAY. Jane and I went to see Mrs Overton's daughter. Mamma and I went out after dinner. I met Kate Mackie at the station. I wrote to Sophy Compson.

21 FRIDAY. Miss Blackwood called. Mamma Kate Mackie & I went into the town with Emily and Jane

22 SATURDAY. Mama Kate, Emily Barron Rose & I went by omnibus to Warwick to be photographed

23 SUNDAY. LES.. *M.*—Pro. 2, Luke 9. *E.*—Pro. 3, Eph. 3.
Went with Mamma to church once. Wet day. Rose and Kate stayed at home

24 MONDAY. Mrs Tarratt the Barrons and Miss Blackwood called

25 TUESDAY. Letter from Sophy Compson. Mama and I went to the post office

26 WEDNESDAY. Miss Blackwood and I walked to Lillington
Kate Mackie and I went to tea at the Barrons

27 THURSDAY. Wet day no going out; Emily and Jane came called on Kate Mackie Rose and Kate went to tea at Miss Blackwoods.

28 FRIDAY. Mamma, Kate, Rose, and I went into the town to buy winter dresses

29 SATURDAY. Our photographs came from Warwick I went to see the Barron's walked out with Emily, lunched there. Dr Bickmore called. Two people came to look at the house

30 SUNDAY. LES. *M.*—Pro. 11, Luke 16. *E.*—Pro. 12, Phil. 4.

To school and church a.m. Kate and I went with the Barrons to Milverton chapel. Mr Parkes preached

Muller is convicted
good morning

31 MONDAY. We all with Miss Blackwood & Jane Barron walked to Guy's Cliff. Emily dined with us Letter from Louisa

Emily cutting out clothes

1 TUESDAY. We all went to church. Into town after lunch to buy trimmings for dress. 2nd vol. of haunted hearts.

Kate Mackie Rose asleep Mama AMP (Haunted Hearts clever book)

2 WEDNESDAY. [Mich. Term begins.]

I called on Emily, went to my district. Emily & Jane called in afternoon

Barron's kitchen and cook

Emily making soup AMP

3 THURSDAY. The Barrons and Alfred Clifton called. We all went into town after an early dinner Miss Dews called

4 FRIDAY. Mrs Mackie & her daughters Charlotte and Grace came to take Kate home. Rose and I went out with them shopping After dinner Rose and I went to buy ribbon

5 SATURDAY. Rose and I went out sp shopping am. Mrs Tarrant called Two families looked over the house.

6 SUNDAY. LES.. *M.*—Pro. 13, Luke 22. *E.*—Pro. 14, 1 Thess. 2.

To church and school. very cold

going to school

7 MONDAY. Rose and I went to see the Barrons thence into the town shopping. Mamma and I called upon the Macgrigors and Mrs Warren. I wrote to Louisa

Mama Mrs M. AMP Miss M.

8 TUESDAY. Went to my district. dined at the Barrons Miss Sandys & Miss Gosselin

Emily's sewing machine

9 WEDNESDAY. [Ld. Mayor's Day. Pr. of Wales b.]

Went out with Rose after luncheon to Miss Bayman

Rose having dress tried on by Miss Bayman

10 THURSDAY. Called on Miss Blackwood into town shopping, The Bakers called for club money Jane came to dine with q

club bag basket book & pencil

11 FRIDAY. [Half-Quarter Day.] Mrs Tarratt called and Miss Blackwood. At home all day braiding my dress

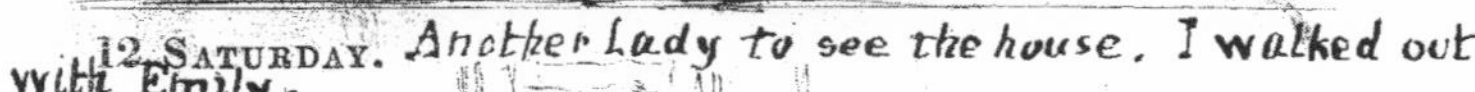

12 SATURDAY. Another Lady to see the house. I walked out with Emily.

13 SUNDAY. LES.. *M.*—Pro. 15, John 5. *E.*—Pro. 16, 1 Tim. 1.
Wetday so did not go to school to church twice,

Müller hanged
14 MONDAY. Warmer and bright. Mama and I went into town called on the Carters and Mrs Wilmore the Mc. grigors, Temples & Miss Gosselin called

15 TUESDAY. Took the money to Miss Baker, went to club. Mama and I called on Mrs Meredith

16 WEDNESDAY. We all walked on the Warwick road I wrote to Louisa. Emily and Jane called A weaver brought some sweet things to sell. Mama ordered a black & gold table cloth

17 THURSDAY. Pouring wet day so stayed at home letter from Louisa I sent Kate Mackie's photograph

The Hill's pig

18 FRIDAY. Wet morning Mama and I went into town called on Miss Blackwood Mrs Dale and Emily called

19 SATURDAY. Emily & Mrs Chapman called, I finished braiding my dress.

20 SUNDAY LES .*M.*—Pro. 17, John 12. *E.*—Pro. 19, 2 Tim. 3.

21 MONDAY. Emily Barron called A letter from Greville to Louisa

22 TUESDAY. Mama and I called on the Pinches & Mrs Cobbe read in the free reading room. Some people came to look at the house

23 WEDNESDAY. Called at the Barrons on my way to Springfield district. Miss Blackwood & Miss Gosselin called The people supposed to have taken the house Emily dined with us.

24 THURSDAY. Worked all day at the books & china I dined with Miss Blackwood. Miss Gosselin & Jane came to tea

25 FRIDAY. Rose [Mich. Term ends.] & I went to Springfield & to Miss Baymens. Mrs Cobbe & Miss Edwardes called I dined at the Barrons. Posted my letter to Greville

26 SATURDAY Mama and I called on the Shiptons. Mrs Tarratt Miss Harris & Gibbs. Emily & Miss Gosselin called

27 SUNDAY. LES.. *M.*—Isaiah 1, John 19. *E.*—Isaiah 2, Hebrews 3.
To school & church twice.

28 MONDAY. Mama and I called upon the Haddons Megrigors, Leighs Warren, Temples, & Carters to bid adieu. Miss Blackwood & Mrs Dale dined with us

Mrs Forsyth AMP Mrs Warren Mama Mrs Megrigor

29 TUESDAY. Went to my district called on Miss Baker & the Pinches & Mrs Cobbe to say adieu. Called at the Barron Jane & Miss Gosselin dined with us

30 WEDNESDAY. Up and down stairs all day packing up The Pinches & Miss Blackwood called

DECEMBER, 1864. Mysie & Miss Andrewes met us at the Bath station

1 THURSDAY. Left Leamington at 8 oclk this morning for Torquay where we arrived at 3.46. had a lovely journey. Louy met us at the station. Dreadfully tired fleas & dirt.

At Bath

Mysie & Miss Andrewes talking to Rose & AMP at window Mamma in foreground

2 FRIDAY. Mama and Louisa went out lodging hunting, and have taken some at 1. Abbey crescent. Miss Bolt & Miss McDougall called and took Rose and me into the town. went to four oclk service at St Lukes

AMP Miss McDougall Mr Taylor. Rose Miss Bolt Belgrave Road

3 SATURDAY We left the loathly lodgings and came to Abbey crescent, much warmer than Clifton Villa. Louisa & I went into the town

4 SUNDAY. LES.. *M.*—Isaiah 5, Acts 5. *E.*—Isaiah 24, Heb. 10.

We all went to St Lukes am. Louisa & I went again in the evening

5 MONDAY. Louisa and I went to the dressmakers at Tor called on Miss Bolt. I wrote to Jane Barron

6 TUESDAY. Louisa and I went to early service at Tor. Mr, Mrs & Miss Taylor, Miss Bolt, & Miss McDougall called. Mamma and I went out afternoon.

7 WEDNESDAY. Arthur went to Plymouth to be examined by the medic men. Rose went to meet Mr Purton at Teignmouth & brought him back to Torquay.

AMP Arthur, Rose in cab

DECEMBER, 1864.

8 THURSDAY. Mama and Louisa put off going out until the bright part of the day had passed so, we got wet through. Arthur came back.

9 FRIDAY. Worked at home all day. Letter from Jane Barron
I wrote to Miss [illegible]kwood

10 SATURDAY. Louisa & I went to the early service. Mama and I walked to Daddy's hole. Mrs Goldstone called

11 SUNDAY. LES.. *M.*—Isaiah 25, Acts 11. *E.*—Isaiah 26, James 4.
We all went to St Lukes morn I went to Tor church afternoon with the Taylors.

12 MONDAY. Miss Taylor and I walked to Ansty's cove am. Miss Bolt & Miss Macdougall called

13 TUESDAY. Louisa and I went with Miss Bolt to a meeting for the S.P.G. in the assembly rooms. nobody particular to speak. got wet through coming home. I wrote to Mysie.

14 WEDNESDAY. The piano arrived from Leamington. I led Mama a dance after the dressmaker's abode, which we found at last.

15 THURSDAY. Louisa & I went to daily prayer at 8am. Letter from Greville to Mama dated Oct. 10th. Mrs Blake called with Miss Bolt.

16 FRIDAY. [Cam. Mich. Term ends.]
Cold east wind; stayed at home all day

17 SATURDAY. [Oxford Mich. Term ends.] Rose's birthday
Arthur, Louisa & I drove to Watcombe, Mama went a drive with Rose & Mr Purton

18 SUNDAY. LES.. *M.*—Isaiah 30, Acts 18. *E.*—Isaiah 32, 2 Peter 1.
We went to St Lukes morn. and afternoon. cold & horrid east wind

Abbey crescent
going to Church

19 MONDAY. Dull day so stayed at home & braided my Jacket
I had a letter from Miss Blackwood

20 TUESDAY. Louisa & I went to early prayers at Tor. Mama
and I returned Mrs Goldstone's & Mrs Blakes calls

Mrs P. AMP.

Paignton road

21 WEDNESDAY. Mama & I walked Arthur & Louisa drove round
the new cut. lovely view.

Miss Gosselin sent me her photograph

22 THURSDAY. Miss Taylor and I walked to Land's end & Daddy's hole Louisa & I had tea with the Taylors & then went with them to a concert at the Mechanic's Institute. Mr Fowler played beautifully on the piano

Toby's leap

Miss McD | AMP | Mrs T | Louisa | Miss T.

biting northeaster.

23 FRIDAY. Mama Louisa and I went into town shopping.

Louisa Mama buying holly AMP Toby

24 SATURDAY. Louisa and I went to early prayers at Tor. I wrote and posted a letter to Jane Barron. Miss McDougal called. Kate Mackie sent us each some pretty work as a christmas box

(Toby) Porch. Torchurch

Mama gave me a waist buckle, Louisa a pair of sleeve studs Rose a garnet ring & Mr Purton a box of chocolate. Miss Blackwood sent me a little book & something pretty to each

DECEMBER, 1864.

25 SUNDAY. bitter cold [Christmas Day.] To St Lukes morn & after(noon)

LES.. *M.*—Isaiah 9 to v. 8, Luke 2 to v. 15.
E.—Isaiah 7 v. 10 to v. 17, Titus 3 v. 4 to 9.

bitter cold 26 MONDAY. The Taylors called. Mama & I went out to look for a green grocers as all the shops are closed found one at last

Letter from Mysie 27 TUESDAY. Finished braiding my jacket and burnt a hole in it as soon as I finished it. Rose Mr Purton and I went to a soiree at the Taylors

28 WEDNESDAY. I and Toby went to the dressmakers, called and had luncheon with Miss Bolt.

warmer than Monday

29 THURSDAY. Louisa and I went to early prayers at Tor. Mamma and I called on the Taylors to St Lukes afterwards

30 FRIDAY. Miss Taylor came to luncheon, she, Louisa and I walked to Meadfoot beach, home by the New cut

north easter

31 SATURDAY. Louisa and I went to early prayers. I walked with Miss Bolt to Marychurch; christmas decorations very good taste

Letters from Miſs Black JANUARY, 1865. wood and Jane Barrow

1 SUNDAY. LES.. *M.*—Isa. 37, Matt. 1. *E.*—Isa. 38, Rom. 1.
We went to St Luke's a.m. Mama Louisa & I went to afternoon service at Cockington

2 MONDAY. Mamma and I went into the town after luncheon caught in the rain.

Lovely day
3 TUESDAY. Went with Loo to early prayers. Mamma Loo & I went into town and down into the bathing cove

4 WEDNESDAY. Louisa and I called at the Taylors went out with Miſs Taylor. Miſs Bourne called through Mrs Wilmore's introduction.

5 THURSDAY. Louy and I went to early prayers. Mr Purton went away by the 9 oclk train. Rose not very lively all day. Louisa & I dashed into the town after luncheon remained there until dark at Louisa's bidding rain and wind.

6 FRIDAY. I went [Epiphany.] to St Luke's a.m. afterwards bought some mincepies for luncheon. walked out with Rose. Rose is livelier! Miss Mc Dougall called. Mamma has a bad cough

lovely
7. SATURDAY. Went with Loo to early prayers. Rose and I walked to Meadfoot sand, on our way home Rose had her
her hair cut short at Jacombs, and was brushed by the machine

8 SUNDAY. LES.. *M.*—Isaiah 44, Mat. 6. *E.*—Isaiah 46, Romans 6.

[Fire Insurance ceases.] To St Luke's a.m. bishop Spencer (Jamaica) preached a gentle good sermon. Mama Louisa & I went to Tor church afternoon. wet.

Mama Loo AMP Tor church

9 MONDAY. Louy & I went to early prayers. Miss Taylor came to practise duetts with Rose and walked afterwards into the town with Mammy & me. We called after luncheon upon Miss Bourne. Rosy & Rose spent the evenining at Miss McDougall's

10 TUESDAY. Mr & Mrs Thompson left Torquay today wished us goodbye. Mr Richards called to sign Arthur's halfpay payers. I went to Hatchers. wet afternoon

11 WEDNESDAY. I wrote [Hilary Term begins.] to Mysie. Louisa & I called on Miss McDougall & the Taylors to St Lukes afterwards

Mama Rose after tea

12 THURSDAY. Dreadfully stormy night, so that neither Miss Bolt or Louisa & I could go to church. I went with Rose to Treeby's to have my hair cut. Louisa and I went to see Miss Bolt & poor old Mrs Willcox; to St Luke's. p.m.

13 FRIDAY. [Cam. Lent Term begins.]

14 SATURDAY. [Ox. Lent Term begins.] Rose and I went to St Luke's pm

JANUARY, 1865.

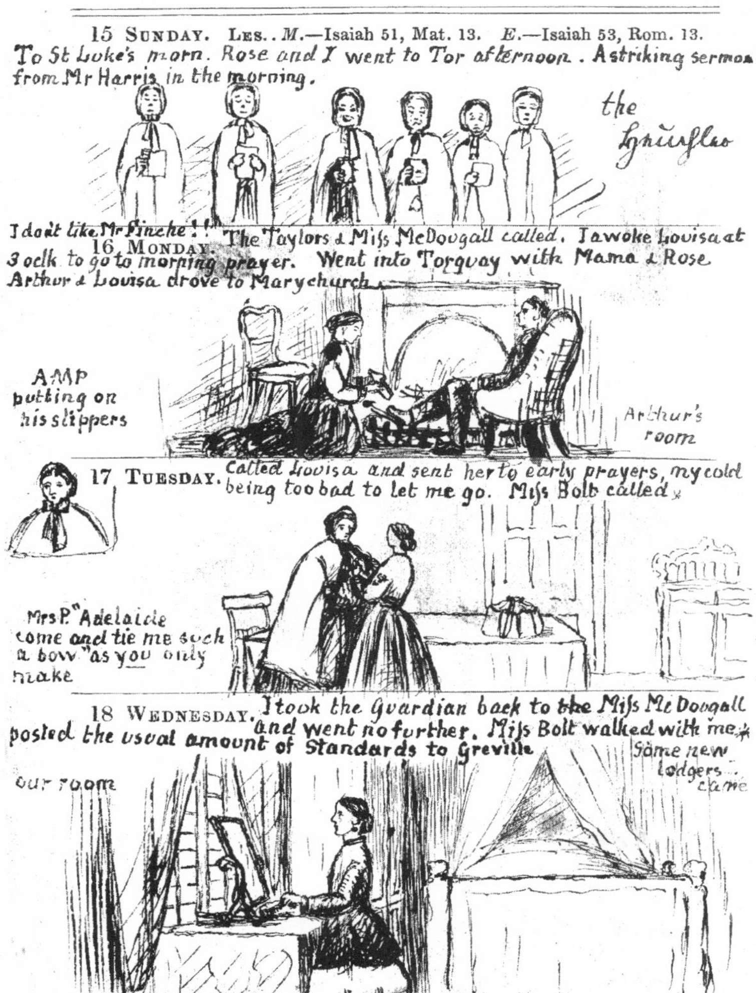

15 SUNDAY. LES.. *M.*—Isaiah 51, Mat. 13. *E.*—Isaiah 53, Rom. 13.
To St Luke's morn. Rose and I went to Tor afternoon. A striking sermon from Mr Harris in the morning.

16 MONDAY. The Taylors & Miss McDougall called. I awoke Louisa at 3 oclk to go to morning prayer. Went into Torquay with Mama & Rose Arthur & Louisa drove to Marychurch.

17 TUESDAY. Called Louisa and sent her to early prayers, my cold being too bad to let me go. Miss Bolt called.

18 WEDNESDAY. I took the Guardian back to the Miss McDougall and went no further. Miss Bolt walked with me. posted the usual amount of Standards to Greville

19 THURSDAY Louisa and I went to morning prayer. Rose and I walked to Meadfoot sands, discovered a lonely rock, up which I shall drag Louisa. Miss Bolt called.

Said to be ye.

Frost 20 FRIDAY. I went to Tor church Miss McDougall lent me some sketches to copy. Miss Taylor & Jack, Louisa, Rose & I walked to Hope's Nose. got covered with mud

Frost!!! 21 SATURDAY. I had a nice long letter from Greville. Mama Louisa and I went into Torquay. very cold.

22 SUNDAY. LES. *M.*—Isa. 55, Matt. 20. *E.*—Isa. 56, 1 Cor. 4.
To St Luke's morn. Mama Louisa & I went to Tor church afternoon

bitter cold
23 MONDAY. Louisa and I went to early prayers we walked after luncheon with Miss Bolt to the cemetry and Chapel hill

Chapel hill
Miss Bolt
Louisa
AMP

24 TUESDAY. Went with Louisa to early prayers. Rose and I went after breakfast into Torquay I had a letter from Mysie

Conversion of St Paul
25 WEDNESDAY. Pouring with rain all day, Mamma and I went to post letters & papers to Greville, got into a ponyfly to come home

26 THURSDAY. Another pouring wet day. Mama and I went into Torquay tired of waiting for better weather.
wrote to Jane

27 FRIDAY. Snow!! Rose and I went into Torquay & Torre. I made a blind for Arthur's room

28 SATURDAY. To early prayers with Louisa. Mama and I walked to Chelston and Cockington. former a most lovely but dilapidated hamlet

29 SUNDAY. LES.. *M.*—Isa. 57, Matt. 26. *E.*—Isa. 58, 1 Cor. 10.

Mama Louisa and I went to St Luke's a.m Mr Harris preached, I always like him. Too stormy to go out again

watching the break-ers

AMP Rose

30 MONDAY. Mama Rose and I went into Torquay I had a note from Sophy Compson.

Mama buying crocus & snowdrops at Prusts Fleet St.

31 TUESDAY. I went [Hilary Term ends.] alone to early prayers Louisa Rose and I went into Torquay after luncheon. rainy. Thund & lightning at night

AMP & Louisa trying to shut Arthur's window

1 WEDNESDAY. Rose & I went into the town & afterwards to the station to regulate our watches. Miss Bolt called

30 THURSDAY. To morning prayer with Louisa. Went with Louisa to see Mrs Willcox thence to St Lukes. Miss Bolt called

Was Pountney thinking of Wilkie or does her brain hitherto so productive supply her with a new branch of her art

31 FRIDAY. To St Lukes. Mr Richards on Elijah. Miss McDougall took me to see an old man to whom I am to read, ran to St Lukes walked afterwards in the avenues with Miss Bolt and Rose

1 SATURDAY. To morning prayer alone. Louisa & I walked to Babbicombe along the cliffs the loveliest & giddiest walk I ever went primroses (the first Ive seen this year) growing over the precipice

Letter from Adeline

"Who can these dear ones be?"

To morning prayer with Louisa. Letter from Mysie.

6 THURSDAY. Mama Louisa & I went into Torquay, to St Lukes Lock. To the post office after with Rose. Forgot Mrs Willcox

7 FRIDAY. [Cam. Lent Term ends.] Did much work. Arthur's birthday Letter from Aunt Julia

8 SATURDAY. [Ox. Lent Term ends. Fire Insur. cea.] I altered dear Louisa's tunnel bonnet

9 SUNDAY. LES.. *M.*—Exo. 9, Matt. 26. *E.*—Exo. 10, Heb. 5 to v. 11.
[Palm Sunday.] To St Luke's morn to Tor alone afternoon.

10 MONDAY. To St Lukes. afterwards to Miss Bolt with Standard, to Mrs Blakes with list of services this week, & to Mrs Willcox Mama Louisa & Rose drove to Broadhempstone, won't do.

11 TUESDAY. To St Lukes. We all went to Betts's to buy springraiment as the "burden of our linseys is greater than we can bear" Wrote to Miss Blackwood. We began to dine early today

12 WEDNESDAY. To St Luke's morn & afternoon. careered about all day with Mama Louisa or Rose Went to Miss Weymouth

13 THURSDAY. To St Lukes morn and even sermon at even Mr Frith. Mama Louisa & I went into Torquay before dinner

14 FRIDAY [Good Friday.]

LES., *M.*—Gen. 22 to v. 20, John 18. *E.*—Isaiah 53, 1 Pet. 2.

To St Luke's morn. Letter from Miss Blackwood

15 SATURDAY. [Easter Term begins.] To St Luke's morn. Went into Torquay before & after dinner with Mama & Louisa to Tor. pm. bought new gloves for tomorrow. new lodgers departed wonder why?

16 SUNDAY. LES.. *M.*—Exo. 12, Rom. 6. *E.*—Exo. 14, Acts 2, v. 22.
[Easter Sunday.] To St Luke's morn & evening Mr Harris preached at night beautiful sermon of course but shall not go again in the evening on account of the heat & Mr Harris will be gone

17 MONDAY. To Tor church at eleven. Mama and I went out after dinner sat in the public gardens

18 TUESDAY. Mama & I went into Torquay shopping before dinner I went to St Luke's 5 oclk. thence to Miss Weymouth. Alone & unassisted I trimmed my hat.

19 WEDNESDAY. Wet day nevertheless out of doors a great deal to St Luke's 5 oclk afterwards into town again with Mamma; in all three drenchings.

The Woodhouse's went by the same train as M. shall miss them at morning prayer

20 THURSDAY. Mama and Arthur went by train to Lower Ebford, the house all we could desire. Louisa Rose & I walked to the bathing cove, read there until dinner time. pleasant. Reading afternoon

Louisa Rose AMD

21 FRIDAY. [Cam. Easter Term begins.] After dinner Mama and I walked to Landsend Miss Bolt called.

AMP Toby Mama

22 SATURDAY. Letter from Myria. To St Luke's 5 oclk, we all walked afterwards into Torquay to help Rose to choose a new hat. find that mine with two ends is vulgar

23 SUNDAY. LES.. *M.*—Numb. 16, Acts 20. *E.*—Numb. 22, 2 Pet. 2.
[Low Sunday.] To St Lukes a.m. Bishop of Jamaica preached forty minutes. To Tor after dinner with Mama, heat great

Mama & AMP in the avenues after church

24 MONDAY. Went into Torquay with Mama. Miss Taylor dined with us, after dinner she Louisa & I walked to the New cut a farewell walk as Miss T goes back to Scotland on Wednesday

Louisa Miss Taylor AMP. New cut

25 TUESDAY. Louisa and I called on the Taylors then walked to Marychurch after a new washerwoman. having dismissed our former one for insolence To St Lukes 5 oclk with Louisa and Rose

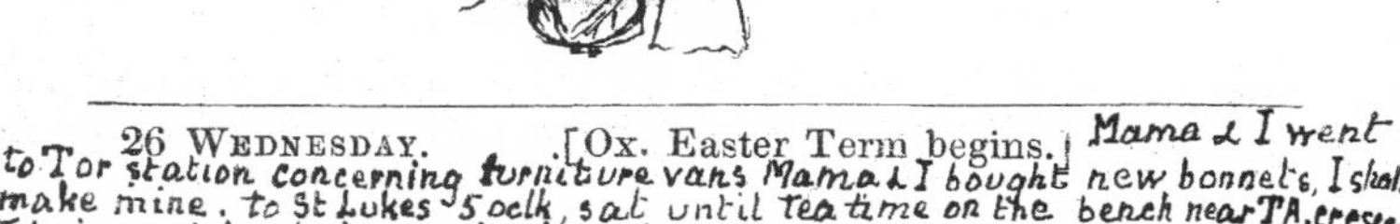

26 WEDNESDAY. [Ox. Easter Term begins.] Mama & I went to Tor station concerning furniture vans Mama & I bought new bonnets, I shall make mine. to St Lukes 5 oclk, sat until tea time on the bench near T.A. cresc. I trimmed Louisa's new Leghorn hat

30 SUNDAY. LES.. *M.*—Num. 23, 24, Acts 27. *E.*—Num. 25, 2, 3 John

To St Lukes morning. too rainy to go again slashed my thumb at dinner in an argument with Rose

1 MONDAY. To St Lukes am and pm. into Torquay. sat on the bench with Mama until teatime

2 TUESDAY. Into Torquay with Rose before dinner To St Lukes 5 oclk, to Seely's library afterwards with Mamma

3 WEDNESDAY. Rainy day, Rose & I went twice into the town We have the refusal of the house at Lower Ebford.

4 THURSDAY. Wet day again yet Rose and I went into Torquay at home the rest of the day We have taken rooms at Livermead Cottage from Saturday week

AMP taking the rooms Miss Matthews

5 FRIDAY. Wet again cleared up at sunset. Mrs Hervey inclined to be insolent about Arthur's soup. Began my drawing again. I gave Toby a beating for jumping through the window

6 SATURDAY. After dinner We all walked to Livermead Cottage to look at a room for Arthur. Into Torquay afterwards to post letters to Blackie etc. the country looks lovely

AMP Mrs P meeting Rose on the strand

14 SUNDAY. LES. *M.*—Deut. 6, Matt. 12. *E.*—Deut. 7, Romans 13.
To St Luke's morn. couldnot manage the afternoon. Mama I & Toby walked on the cliffs very pleasant

15 MONDAY. Letter from Emy. Rose & I walked into Torquay wet thro coming back. Rose & I sat on the rocks after dinner

16 TUESDAY. Mrs Blake & Miss Bolt called. I wrote to Emy went out for a little upon the small sands too windy to be pleasant Rose has taken to sea anemones.

Troubadour. AMP Rose.

17 WEDNESDAY. Have a cough so stayed in bed all day

Do you remember my brother, Cook?

21 SUNDAY. LES.. *M.*—Deut. 8, Matt. 19. *E.*—Deut. 9, 1 Cor. 1.
[Rogation Sunday.] To Cockington church am with Mama L. & R. Lanes most lovely

22 MONDAY. On the cliffs until dinner Into Torquay & to St Lukes after dinner with Mamma & Rose

23 TUESDAY. Wrote to Mysie Colonel Jackson called We have taken his house at Ebford from Michaelmas next

24 WEDNESDAY. [Queen Victoria born, 1819.] On the cliffs all day Mr Goldstone came to sound my lungs. Miss Bolt called

25 THURSDAY. [Ascension. Trinity Term begins.]
On the cliffs again until teatime. Am beginning to be tired of the contemplative life quite alone, and shall not be sorry for an active hour, for a little contrast

26 FRIDAY. Mr Goldstone came again to see me, Mrs G called on the cliffs all day. Louisa overtaken by the tide, coming out of Thunder Hole

27 SATURDAY. Louisa & I sat on the sands am Miss Bolt called brought me some Sunday books for tomorrow. Henry Purton wants to marry Rose in August

8 THURSDAY. Rose took me into Torquay to post her letter I found out a new milkman. home through the avenues. On the cliffs after dinner.

near the avenues

9 FRIDAY. Letter from Blackie. Mamma and I walked into Torquay after dinner to enquire for domestics home in a pony fly.

Fisher's shop

10 SATURDAY. Mama engaged a little housemaid this morn. Mama & I spent the afternoon on the cliffs

In the arbour

11 SUNDAY. LES.. *M.*—Gen. 1, Matt. 3. *E.*—Gen. 18, 1 John 5.
[Trinity Sunday.] To Cockington in the morning. Watched the mackerel fishing

12 MONDAY. On the sands a.m. Louisa & I went into Torquay shopping I bought a new Leghorn hat like Louisa's Wrote to Blackie

13 TUESDAY Rose & I trimmed my hat. Mama Louisa & I went into Torquay I walked back M & L drove in a pony fly the road like a furnace. We sat on the cliffs after dinner

14 WEDNESDAY. Started to go into the town with Mama returned by the shore with Louisa broke my umbrella on the rocks & tore my dress After dinner Louisa & I called to invite Mrs Blake to luncheon. Wrote to Adeline

15 THURSDAY. [Trinity Term ends.] Mamma and I called on Miss Bolt went into Torquay, before dinner. On the cliffs after dinner with M.

Pountney must have ... when painting this marine subject

H.M.S Saint George 90 guns

16 FRIDAY. Letter from Maria I stayed on the cliffs all day because the sun has scorched my face

17 SATURDAY. About the cliffs morn. Mama and I went into Torquay after dinner drove home in a pony fly

To procure sleep. One teaspoonful of magnesia with a few drops of heartshorn or sal volatile mixed in water

JUNE, 1865.

18 SUNDAY. LES.. *M.*—Joshua 10, Luke 2. *E.*—Joshua 23, Gal. 2.

To Cockington as usual morn. Mama Louisa & I went to Tor church, even

19 MONDAY. Letter from Minnie Walker. Into Torquay morn & afternoon to post papers to Greville Mrs Blake & Miss Bolt came to luncheon

20 TUESDAY. [Accession Queen Victoria.

Louisa & I went to Miss Bolts to bring away our drums

21 WEDNESDAY. [Proclamation Queen Victoria.]

Packed up my trunk Mama Louisa & I went into Torquay after dinner to put off cook, housmaid, & Pickford's van for luggage until Saturday as we do not go to Ebford until then

In cases of cramp, a towel dipped in hot water and applied to the part affected, will procure relief.

JUNE, 1865.

22 THURSDAY. On the cliffs two hours, Louisa & I packed the bath After dinner she and I went to St Lukes post office & Miss Weymouth home through the lovely avenues I wrote to Minnie Walker

23 FRIDAY. [Cam. Easter Term ends.]
I went after dinner to Luscombes (butcher) for meat for beeftea Arthur still ill in bed

24 SATURDAY. [Midsummer Day.]
Louisa & I went a walk in the loveliest lanes & country I ever saw. After dinner went with L. to St Lukes gave Miss Bolt bag and books Finished packing the hampers. I wonder if Maria will send me a cadeau tomorrow

Eggs may be preserved a month by boiling them for one minute, or, steep them in sweet oil for a time

JUNE, 1865.

25 SUNDAY. LES. *M.*—Judges 4, Luke 8. *E.*—Judges 5, Eph. 2.

Mama & I went to ask Mr Bradin to go down to see Arthur who is still weak & out of sorts. To St Lukes afterwards. Mama L. & I went to Torre in the evening. Obliged to finish packing as we go to Ebford tomorrow

Letter from Essy, Mysie

26 MONDAY.

Mama Rose & I came by 8 oclk train to our new house at Ebford one van of furniture came followed by the other later. house just what we want. Arthur & Louisa came after dinner with Toby The two maidservants came with us

27 TUESDAY.

I, unassisted, dusted, and arranged all the books in the library between breakfast and tea The grate is being put in the drawingroom Mama & Rose went into Topsham to discover shops etc

28 WEDNESDAY. [Queen Victoria crowned, 1838.]

Still in a whirl, some of the pictures hung today, clock put up etc

The Lancet states that an infusion of wild thyme will, in many cases of whooping cough, remove the complaint when other remedies fail

29 THURSDAY. I wrote to Emy Put the diningroom tidy the drawingroom pictures hung

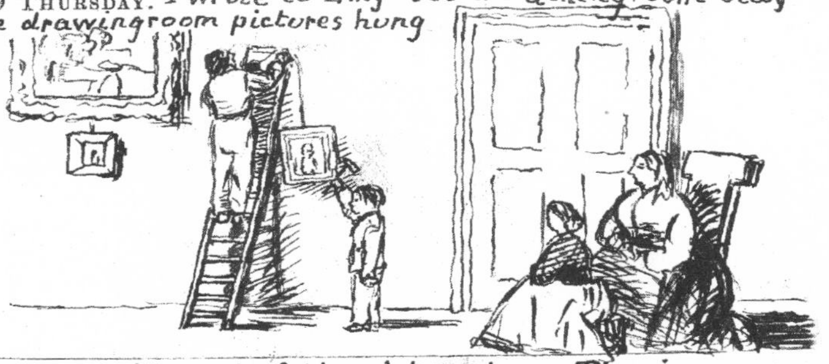

30 FRIDAY. The rest of the pictures hung. The piano came

We are reminded in this domestic scene of Teniers

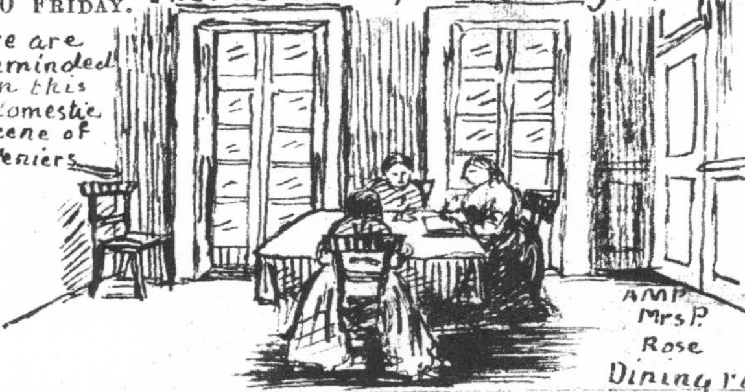

AMP
Mrs P.
Rose
Diningroom

1 SATURDAY. Mama & Louisa went to shop at Exeter, I walked with them to Topsham went down to the river along the strand, a quaint straggling street on the riverside, Topsham is an ugly town with the most hideous church I ever saw
it is a most picturesque town.

LP Mrs P AMP. The Ex

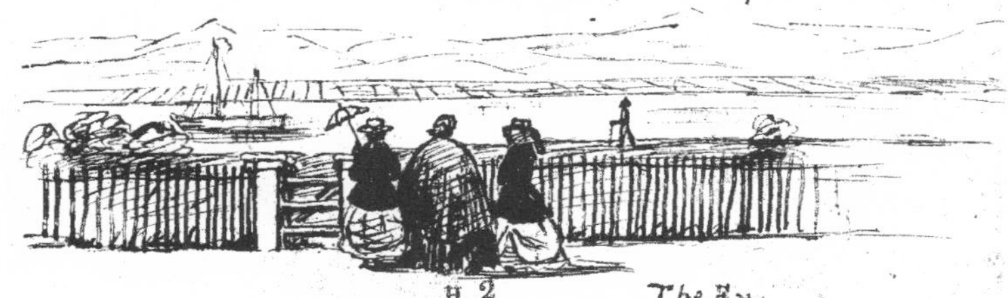

Letter from Emy

2 SUNDAY. LES.. *M.*—1 Sam. 2, Luke 14. *E.*—1 Sam. 3, Phil. 2.

Mama Rose & I drove in Casely's fly to Woodbury, our parish church Mr Fulford clergyman. Service intoned [illegible] & Louisa & I went - after dinner to Clyst St George. being nearer than Woodbury

3 MONDAY. Mama & I walked to hideous Topsham along the still more ugly road, to get tables, garden tools etc A woman cutting & fitting the carpets

4 TUESDAY. Rather showery, so stayed at home Wrote to Emy. Bedroom carpets put down

5 WEDNESDAY. Louisa & I went after a dreſsmaker at St George's Clyst. country prettier than we thought. Miſs Lee, Col. Jackson & Miſs Hayman called

6 THURSDAY. *Cough bad again*

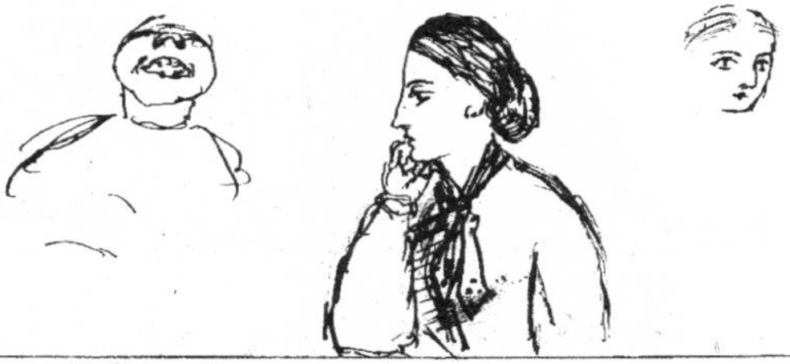

7 FRIDAY. *Ditto*

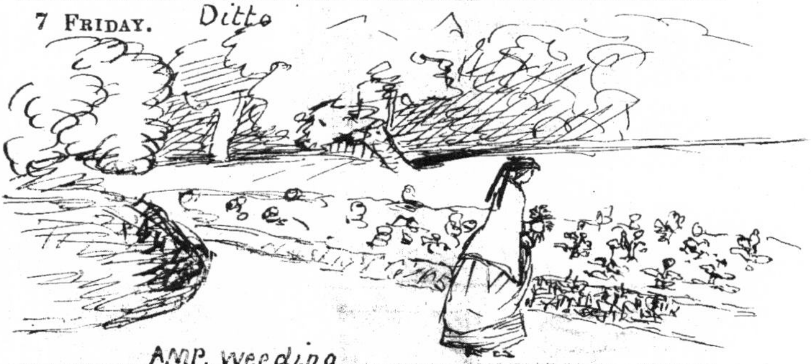

AMP. Weeding

8 SATURDAY. [Ox. Trin. T. ends. Fire Insur. cea.]
Rose and I walked in the lanes after the showers had subside lanes very pretty

Lympstone road Rose AMP.
The Exe in the distance

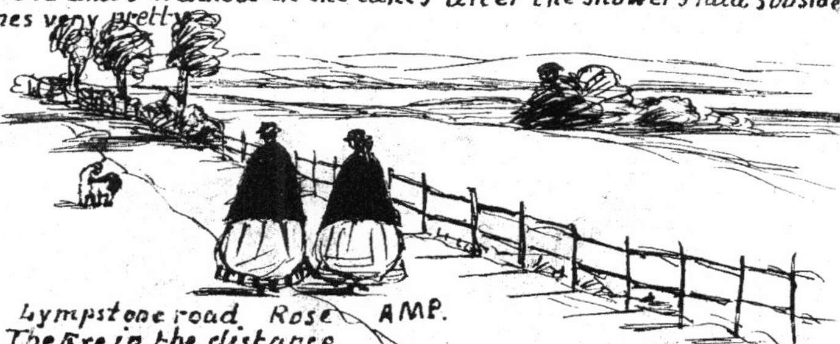

9 SUNDAY. LES.. *M.*—1 Sam. 12, Luke 21. *E.*—1 Sam. 13, 1 Thes. 1.
Mama Louisa Rose & I went to Woodbury in Casely's fly would not walk Letter from Aunt Julia

10 MONDAY. Mr & Mrs Fulford & son called I walked out in the lanes alone for fresh air I wrote to Maria & Aunt Julia

11 TUESDAY. cold bad still

12 WEDNESDAY. The Miss Mackie's called & brought Kate (who is staying with them at Exmouth) to spend the day with us
Mem. not to have custards for desert another time

Louisa K.M AMP

Maria won't come to Roses wedding, rude girl!

JULY, 1865.

13 THURSDAY. Wet day. Pratised music, worked, drew, read the livelong day. Cough better again

14 FRIDAY. Rose & I walked into Topsham discovered a new walk, down by the river, where we tasted sea air, to Riversmeet Terrace; saw many of the mop species of Elms, peculiar to this neighbourhood. Pretty view of river

15 SATURDAY. [St. Swithin.] Letter from Aunt Julia. Emy writes to Louisa that she sails for Queensland in Sept. Mama Rose & I called on the Fulfords. Toby went too. I wrote to Maria. Louisa & I are going to take classes at the Sunday school

Mrs M. Rose a friend AMP Mama

16 SUNDAY. LES. M.—1 Sam. 15, John 4. E.—1 Sam. 17, 2 Thes. 3.
All went to Woodbury church drove home by Nutwell. Louisa & I went afterdinner to St George's Clyst, found a new pleasant walk afterwards

17 MONDAY. Mama & I went to Exeter just time to peep into the cathedral and Guildhall nice old town lovely shops, left half our errands undone, home by eight train. Mr & Mrs Ellacombe called while we were away

18 TUESDAY. Showery. Louisa & I fed the pigs for want of some outdoor amusement. Sideboard & table arrived. I wrote to Maria

19 WEDNESDAY. Letter from Maria. Rose did not go to Exmouth to spend the day with Kate Mackie because of the rain

Gladstone turned out of Oxford

20 THURSDAY. Mama & Rose went by train to Exmouth to return the Miss Mackies call. Louisa & I walked to St George's Clyst. Mrs & Miss More, Miss Lee Miss Pennel & Miss Hayman called

Toby under bridge

21 FRIDAY. Too hot to go beyond the garden. Looked at old bits of wool & decided upon making something out of them

Dressing room

22 SATURDAY. At home all day. Capt. Hopper called. The drawing room glass had its top cut off by Hunn of Topsham at Arthurs suggestion saving thereby 4 or 5£.

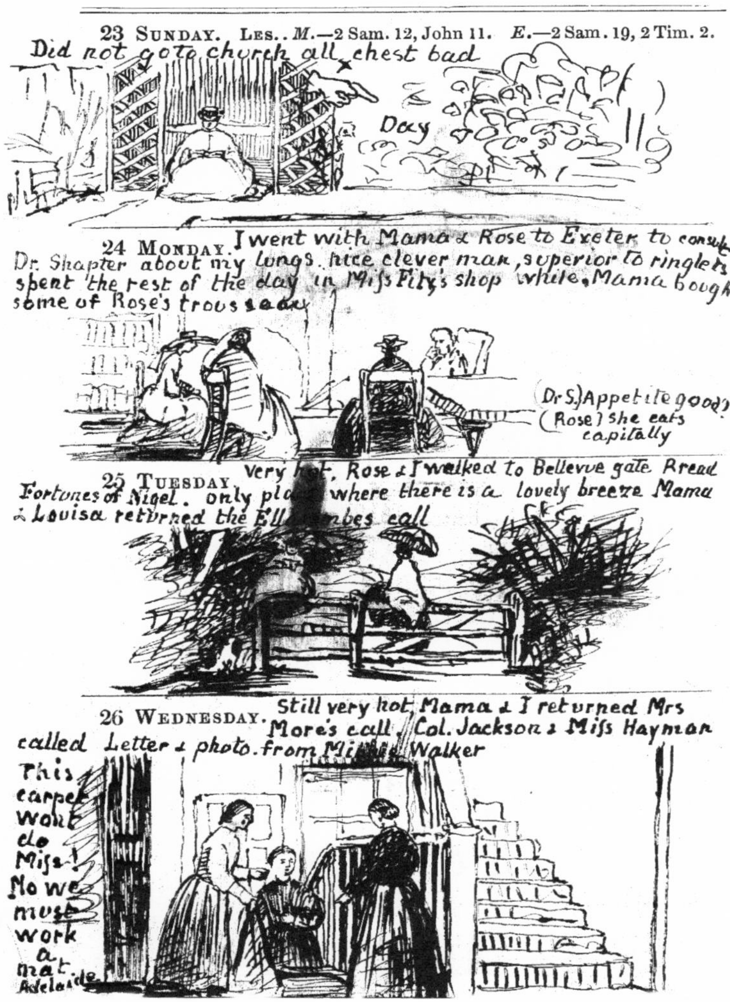

23 SUNDAY. LES.. *M.*—2 Sam. 12, John 11. *E.*—2 Sam. 19, 2 Tim. 2.

Did not go to church all chest bad

Day

24 MONDAY. I went with Mama & Rose to Exeter to consult Dr. Shapter about my lungs. nice clever man, superior to ringlets spent the rest of the day in Miss Fitz's shop while Mama bought some of Rose's trousseau

25 TUESDAY. Very hot. Rose & I walked to Bellevue gate & read Fortunes of Nigel. only place where there is a lovely breeze Mama & Louisa returned the Ell[illegible]mbes call

26 WEDNESDAY. Still very hot, Mama & I returned Mrs More's call. Col. Jackson & Miss Hayman called Letter & photo. from Mi[illegible] Walker

constance Kent not to be hanged but sent to Australia for life

JULY, 1865.

Dr Pritchard hanged on Thursday

27 THURSDAY. Very hot. Louisa & I found out a new walk down to the river, tide out of course, leaving the bed of the Ex like a field of mud, nice breeze too late to see the express go down

28 FRIDAY. Cooler weather. Mr & Mrs Hole called. Rose & I went at last to Russells the dairy
Mama's birthday

29 SATURDAY. Mama & I returned Capt. Hopper's call at Nut-well. We need no longer be ashamed of our locked gates as his were locked [illegible]

30 SUNDAY. LES.. *M.*—2 Sam. 21, John 18. *E.*—2 Sam. 24, Heb. 2.
Arthur & I stayed at home morn. because of the bad weather
To St George's Clyst afternoon with Mama & Louisa

31 MONDAY. Rain all day stayed at home working at Rose's trousseau. Wonder when Maria is coming!

1 TUESDAY Miss More [Lammas Day.] & Mrs Welland called

2 WEDNESDAY. Letter from Mysie who is coming on Saturday
Dr & Mrs Brent called. 3 chicks hatched

3 THURSDAY. The two figures arrived for lighting the hall. The Paragon Phillips brought the boarding to put up before the palings in the garden. I wrote to Mysie. Toby killed the remaining pheasant.

4 FRIDAY. Letter from Blackie. Rose & I called at the Lee's. Col. Jackson & his two nephews Messrs Morris called here. Walked in the lanes with Mama & Rose.

5 SATURDAY. Dear Maria came at last.

6 SUNDAY. LES.. *M.*—1 Kgs. 13, Acts 4. *E.*—1 Kgs. 17, Heb. 9.
Too wet for Arthur & me to go to Church

7 MONDAY. I worked in the garden. Mama & Rose returned Mrs Welland's call

8 TUESDAY. Mama Mysie Louisa & I drove to Woodbury Common lovely air. returned the Brents & Hole's call

9 WEDNESDAY. Mysie Rose & I went to hear Dr Russell play the Organ at General Lee's. afterwards to a croquet party at the Brents

10 THURSDAY. Arthur went to Plymouth Mama & I went same time to Exeter tired ourselves out, went to Dr Shapter Mama lost her purse at Exeter

11 FRIDAY. [Half-Quarter Day.]

12 SATURDAY. In bed all day

13 SUNDAY LES.. *M.*—1 Kgs. 18, Acts 11. *E.*—1 Kgs. 19, James 3.

dull nothing

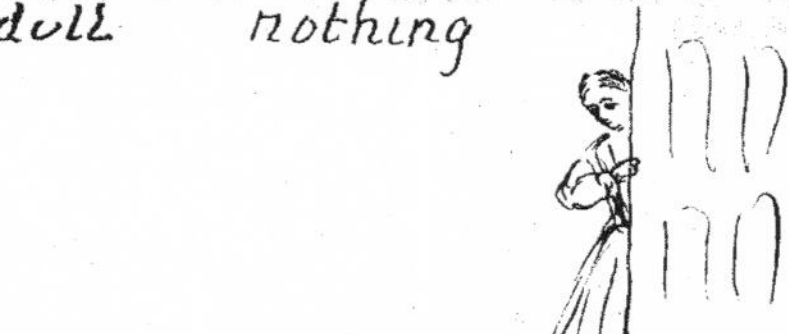

14 MONDAY. Dull again Miss Lee & Hayman called.

15 TUESDAY. Emy is coming this week I wrote to Minnie Walker

16 WEDNESDAY. Mysie & I walked out in the morning caught in a shower, severely treated by family in consequence

17 THURSDAY. Mysie & I walked round the house darenot go farther for fear of rain. Counted the wall fruit four pears gone!

18 FRIDAY. Emy came today

19 SATURDAY. Emy Mysie Louisa & I went to a croquet party at the Fulfords very pleasant

20 SUNDAY. LES.. *M.*—1 Kgs. 21, Acts 18. *E.*—1 Kgs. 22, 1 Pet. 5.
Rain all day Mama Arthur Mysie & I stayed at home all day

21 MONDAY. Weather doubtful so did not go beyond the garden weeded some of the beds. The Croquet set came at last!

Two boxes Miss from Exeter

22 TUESDAY. Mama Louisa & Rose went to Exeter. Mr Tothill came to see Arthur. Capt. Hopper called. Emy & I accompanied Maria on her sketching expedition

sauve qui peut

St George's Clyst

23 WEDNESDAY. Wet day. not too bad for croquet. Miss More called. Louisa's hair dressed horn fashion by Emy, makes her rather self conscious

24 THURSDAY. Fine day. The well was opened and almost poisoned us with bad smell- Croquet. Louisa & I don't improve. Emy sketched our house for Greville.

25 FRIDAY. Mama Emy Mysie Louisa & I went by train to Exmouth dull place, tide miles out

26 SATURDAY. Mr & Mrs Tothill called. Miss Hayman came to play croquet in the afternoon

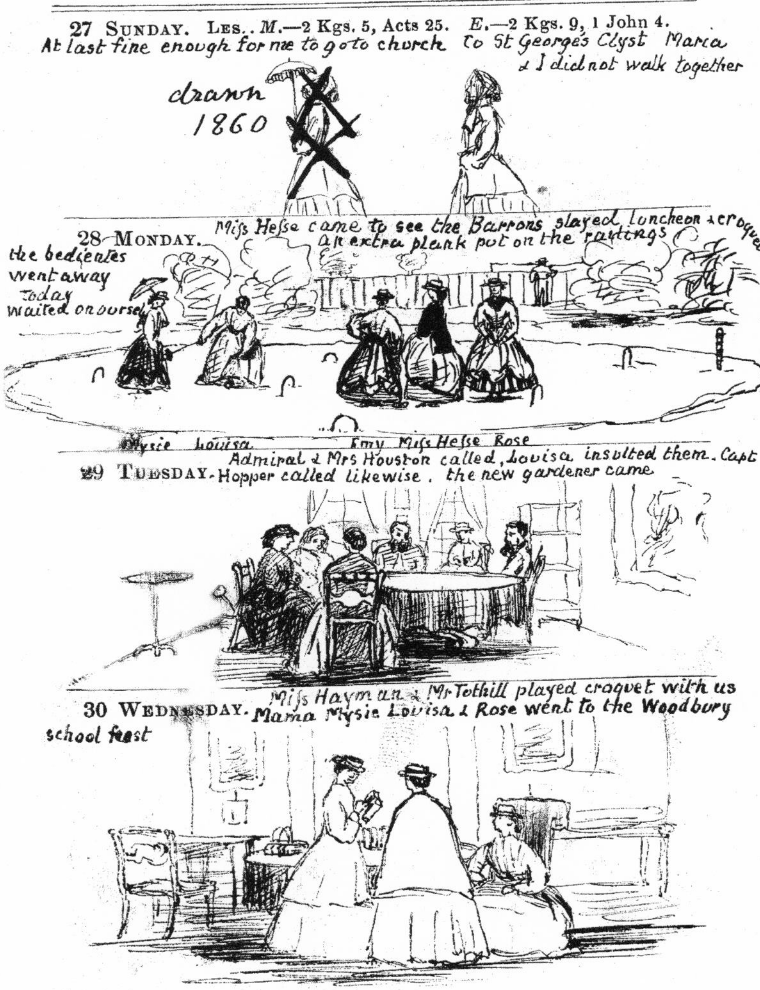

27 SUNDAY. LES.. *M.*—2 Kgs. 5, Acts 25. *E.*—2 Kgs. 9, 1 John 4.
At last fine enough for me to go to church to St George's Clyst Maria & I did not walk together

28 MONDAY. Miss Hesse came to see the Barrons stayed luncheon & croquet an extra plank put on the railings
the bedientes went away today waited on ourselves

29 TUESDAY. Admiral & Mrs Houston called, Louisa insulted them. Capt Hopper called likewise. the new gardener came

30 WEDNESDAY. Miss Hayman & Mr Tothill played croquet with us Mama Mysie Louisa & Rose went to the Woodbury school feast

AUGUST & SEPTEMBER, 1865.

3 SUNDAY. LES.. *M.*—2 Kgs. 10, Matt. 4. *E.*—2 Kgs. 18, Rom. 4.
Too threatening for my church in the morn. Went alone to St Georges p.m.

The great AMP herself

4 MONDAY. Went [illegible] with Mysie sketching very hot played croquet together after luncheon. I won! Mama & the rest went to Capt Hoppers for Emy to milk his cows

Emy Mama their farewell walk in evening

5 TUESDAY. Emy went away this morning Mama & Louisa went with her to Exeter, L & I gave Emy a willow pattern dinner service to take to Australia. (Croquet) Walked with Mysie & Rose to sketch cottage

Emy

6 WEDNESDAY. Croquet as usual. Mama & I returned the Houston's call, not at home.

crossing the line home

7 THURSDAY. Captain Hopper brought his children to play croquet tea in the arbour

8 FRIDAY. Mama and I returned the Tothill's call went into Topsham shopping hunted up Mrs Anis, Rose's workwoman

A Prout. Shapter Street Topsham

9 SATURDAY. Dear Myriar went away this morning Louisa & Rose drove with her to Exeter, I, as far as Topsham. Mama and I called on Mrs More. Miss Lee & Miss Hayman called
The pigs had their noses rung didn't seem to mind but enjoyed some apples I gave them.

10 SUNDAY. LES.. *M.*—2 Kgs. 19, Matt. 11. *E.*—2 Kgs. 23, Rom. 11.
To St George's Clyst am with Louisa. Louisa has taken a class at Woodbury.

Louisa

Letter from Myse
11 MONDAY. Mama & I went to Exeter to look at carriages Capt. Hopper went with us bought Rose's wedding cake

Letter from Blackie
12 TUESDAY. Posted into Topsham with Rose called at the Tothill to ask Mr Tothill to sign a deed. Louisa & I called on Mrs Welland & Miss Ellacombe nicht zu Hause oppressive blackberries good on the road to St George's decided upon one of the pony carriages we saw yesterday & sent Charles to fetch it from Exeter Now for a perfect pony!

Louisa

13 WEDNESDAY. Arthur & I drove to Lympstone very pretty drive, trees reminded me of Warwickshire began copying a drawing for Rose

14 THURSDAY. Drew all day Miss Hayman came to play croquet after luncheon. high wind all day Answered a note of Emy's

15 FRIDAY. Mama & Louisa & I drove to Exeter, the Phaeton unsound on the side where Louisa sat. Mem. not to drive four again if possible. Mama was photographed by de Nicevill called at Mr Tothills on our way back Topsham.

coming home at a butchers pace

16 SATURDAY. Sent the Phaeton back as it is broken to pieces I wrote to Mysie. worked much.

17 SUNDAY. LES.. *M.*—Jer. 5, Matt. 18. *E.*—Jer. 22, 1 Cor. 2.
To St George's morn & afternoon

18 MONDAY. Mr Fulford & Capt Hopper called Letter from Emy

19 TUESDAY. I walked into Topsham to ask Mrs Houston to chaperon us tomorrow Called at the Lee's with Rose Mama & Louisa went to Exeter

20 WEDNESDAY. Louisa Rose & I went to an achery & croquet party at Capt Hoppers Lovely tea Supper, all archers except us, Mrs Houston & the Brown family

21 THURSDAY. Higher wind drew all day beef very salt at dinner, all thirsty tonight

go out Toby

22 FRIDAY. Capt Hopper called to offer to settle the phaeton matter at Exeter. Miss Hayman called brought grapes for Arthur.

I wrote to Emy

23 SATURDAY. Mama & Louisa went to Exeter. Rose & I stayed at home.

AMP Arthur smoking room

24 SUNDAY. LES.. *M.*—Jer. 35, Matt. 25. *E.*—Jer. 36, 1 Cor. 9.
To St George's Clyst morn. & even.

25 MONDAY. Capt Hopper & Daisy & Miss More called. Rose & I walked into Topsham lovely day
The new phaeton came at last

26 TUESDAY. Mama Louisa & Rose drove to Exeter. I stayed at home Louisa ordered me very salt beef for dinner Walked to St George's Clyst lovely day
Emy sailed today for Queensland

children at St George's

27 WEDNESDAY. The horse did not come. Rose & I called at the Lees to invite some of them on Rose's wedding Looked at all their ancestors picture

The Lee's staircase
Miss Lee
AMP
Miss Hayman
Rose
old portrait of twins

28 THURSDAY. Edith Jones & Evans cannot come next week nobody can come Miss Lee & Miss Hayman called. The new horse came, a sweet little creature just suits the phaeton.

29 FRIDAY. Rose [Michaelmas Day.] drove me to Woodbury com ought to be a lovely view, but was too hazy

30 SATURDAY. Col Jackson Miss Hayman & Capt Hopper called. I walked into Topsham Rose drove Arthur out in the phaeton

Dr Jones of Heidelberg memory, has written a sweet letter to Rose of congratulation on her marriage

OCTOBER, 1865.

1 SUNDAY LES.. *M.*—Ezekiel 2, Mark 4. *E.*—Ezekiel 13, 1 Cor. 16.
[Cam. Mich. Term begins.] At home morn. went with Louisa & Rose to Clyst St George afternoon

2 MONDAY. Louisa rushed off to Exeter to do some last errands Mr Wrottesley, Edith Jones, Henry & W. Purton arrived before dinner. directed envelopes in evening.

After dinner

W Purton Louisa Edith AMP directing cards

Rose's presents at Woodbury

3 TUESDAY. Rose & Henry Purton were married today by Mr Wrottesley. Louisa & I bridesmaids. After breakfast Rose & Henry went away to spend some days at Bideford. The Fulfords Capt Hopper & Daisy Hopper & Miss Harman stayed until evening, croquet etc

See Red Book for today

4 WEDNESDAY. Tired. sent off the wedding cards then croquet Mr Wrottesley Edith & Louisa drove to Woodbury

Mr W. Louisa AMP Edith

5 THURSDAY. Mr Wrottesley went away this morning. Miss Lee & Mi[ss] Pennel called

AMP & Edith feeding the lovely Damian in his stable

6 FRIDAY. I drove Edith to Lympstone after luncheon The Fulfords, Ellacombes, & Capt Hopper called

Edith AMP.

7 SATURDAY. Mr & Mrs Tothill called Mama Edith & Louisa we[nt] to croquet at the Fulfords. I wrote to Blackie

OCTOBER, 1865.

8 SUNDAY. LES.. *M.*—Ezekiel 14, Mark 11. *E.*—Ezekiel 18, 2 Cor. 7.
Rain come at last so stayed at home morn. Went to St George, afternoon with Louisa & Edith

going to Church

9 MONDAY. Encore la pluie cleared up after dinner I drove Mama & Edith through Lympstone without Charles

view from Withecombe road

10 TUESDAY. [Oxford Mich. Term begins.] Mama & Louisa went to Exeter. too damp to go beyond the garden Wrote to Mysie

11 WEDNESDAY. Rain & wind Miss More Col Jackson & Miss Hayman called. Could not go out. Postman obliged to wear a Makintosh

Potter

12 THURSDAY. [Fire Insurance ceases.]
Did nothing all day Mrs Welland called.
Mrs Welland
AMP
13 FRIDAY. More industrious, drew much. Nobody called. Louisa took Edith to Topsham a.m. got wet through, & drove Mm out after dinner in fog & damp lighted fires for the first time
Louisa Edith AMP.
le premier feu de l'hiver
14 SATURDAY. Still too damp to go out Mr & Mrs Hole called
Toby shaved & washed by the Post-man's son
Oh my Toby what a fright you are
& what a beauty you were

OCTOBER, 1865.

OCTOBER, 1865

partial eclipse of the sun this afternoon not seen at Ebford

19 THURSDAY. The Portons refused to stay until to morrow & departed at halfpast nine for Exeter in the phaeton. Edith & I walked into Topsham, high wind, took my drawing to Hunns to be framed Miss Ellacombe called to ask us to go to the S.P.G. meeting tonight, did not go

20 FRIDAY. Letter from Blackie, nothing of any consequence occurred beyond walking in the garden. Louisa drove Mama & Edith out, & brought them home safe

21 SATURDAY. Wet day could not walk in the garden nobody went anywhere Edith & Louisa walked out in the damp & twilight Wrote a line of remonstrance to Maria Mama had letter from Rose delighted with her home

22 SUNDAY. LES. M.—Daniel 3, Luke 8. E.—Daniel 6, Eph. 2.

One of the wettest days we have had this year no one went to Church even Louisa stayed at home

My dear Louy you are surely not dreaming of going out in this awful rain!
Oh dear Mama it is quite lovely, so fresh & cool, I could not possibly get wet don't stop me please or I shall be late

23 MONDAY.

Damp still M[illegible] is su[illegible] who [illegible]. Louisa drove Mama & Edith out in the damp

24 TUESDAY.

Weather capricious Edith went away today [illegible] Mr Tothill came to see Arthur

Louisa bought a tie, boots sleeves slippers for herself says I don't want them [illegible]

25 WEDNESDAY.

Papers from a[illegible] Tremendous wind in the night

Wrote to Greville

Look on this picture

23 THURSDAY.

24 FRIDAY.

25 SATURDAY [Michaelmas Term ends.]

The Pristons went away
Letter from Rebekah P

26 SUNDAY. LES.. *M.*—Prov. 13, John 18. *E.*—Prov. 14, Heb. 2.

Mamma & Louisa went to Woolbury

27 MONDAY. Mamma & Louisa drove to Exeter

28 TUESDAY. Capt H called

29 WEDNESDAY. Mamma Louisa & I drove to Honiton Clyst. Letter from H Walker

30 THURSDAY.

1 FRIDAY. Tout le monde called saw none being at dinner A year today since we left Leamington!

2 SATURDAY. Mamma Louisa & I drove to Lympstone home through Woodbury Capt H came in the evening

28 THURSDAY. Rainy so nobody went out

29 FRIDAY. Rainy again. Bad headache all day. Wrote to nobody as I had intended doing. Wonder when I can go out of doors again

30 SATURDAY. I started in a gleam of sunshine to go to Topsham but sent back at once by the rain. Wrote to Aunt Julia

31 SUNDAY. LES.. *M.*—Isaiah 37, Acts 28. *E.*—Isaiah 38, Jude.

Too wet for me to go to church
goodby 1865

3 SUNDAY. LES.. *M.*—Isaiah 1, Acts 4. *E.*—Isaiah 2, Heb. 9.

No church for me Louisa went to St Georges afternoon Dreadful day

4 MONDAY. Dreadful day the Heath flooded. Began German again

5 TUESDAY. Wet again Mama & Louisa managed a drive after dinner

6 WEDNESDAY. Worse than ever torrents of rain. Devonshire winter!! continued my education

7 THURSDAY. Fine at last! Walked to Topsham. Wrote to Rose Mamma & Louisa drove out after dinner

8 FRIDAY. Wet again! German again in consequence Marmion

9 SATURDAY. At ten oclk Mama & Louisa started for Exeter, returned at five (Alone). They brought back some stale buns & cheesecakes

10 SUNDAY. LES.. *M.*—Isaiah 5, Acts 10. *E.*—Isaiah 24. James 3.
We went to Woodbury morn.
Tolerable weather

11 MONDAY. Col Jackson the Morris's & Miss Henry called.
I began German on a new plan

12 TUESDAY. Letter from Myrie Mamma and I walked to St Marys Clyst

13 WEDNESDAY. Mamma & Louise drove to Exeter I walked with Toby to St Marys Clyst

14 THURSDAY. Fine again to Topsham with Louisa bought some baskets at the door

15 FRIDAY. Fine again no one went out all day because I stayed at home cht selmoralle dellac

16 SATURDAY. [Cam. Mich. Term ends.]
Noone went out of doors White frost and fog with cold
Letter from Rose

I made them friends of ...

17 SUNDAY. LES.. *M.*—Isaiah 25, Acts 17. *E.*—Isaiah 26, 1 Peter 5.

No church for me Mamma & Louisa went to St George's

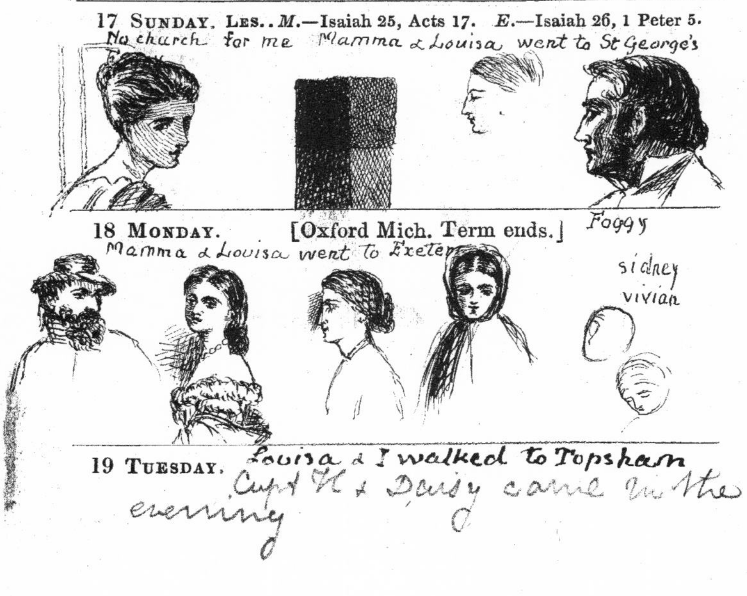

18 MONDAY. [Oxford Mich. Term ends.]

Mamma & Louisa went to Exeter

19 TUESDAY. Louisa & I walked to Topsham

Capt H & Daisy came in the evening

20 WEDNESDAY. Mama Louisa & I spent the day at the Fulfords, helped in the decorations for the Church

21 THURSDAY. Went with Louisa to see Mrs Wellands lovely altarcloth which she has just worked called afternoon on Mr Moore

22 FRIDAY. Mama & Louisa went to Exeter. Miss Skinner was insolent to my dear Louisa

23 SATURDAY. Worked at decorations for Woodbury all day long until 10 at night. am tired

Adelaide's Diary – Notes

1864

2 January 'Mr Purton called in abend [the evening].' Adelaide occasionally ventures into foreign languages in the diary. Even for a leisured lady of her day, she seems to have been unusually determined to widen her knowledge. In 1864 she concentrated on Greek and drawing classes. She took up German again at the end of 1865.

9 February 'To clothing club district.' In 1864 Adelaide devoted almost one day a week to this clothing club, occasionally referring to it as 'Springfield District'. Springfield Street (now known as Shrubland Street) was an especially deprived district of Leamington Spa. The club apparently raised money to clothe the poor. There are sketches on 24/5/64 and 17/9/64 of the club at work, and of the club 'bag, basket, book & pencil' on 10/10/64, but no references to how and from whom they collected the money. Nor is there any suggestion that they collected or handed out clothing. There are frequent references to taking the money to Miss Baker, who must have acted as treasurer. The club may have had a even wider remit (see note on 30/6/64).

27 February 'Mamma and I went to the church to choose a pew.' Nineteenth-century parish churches derived part of their income from 'pew rents'. Some of those who attended Sunday services regularly – and even the not so regular attenders – would pay for the exclusive use of particular pews. From subsequent entries – especially that of 21/8/64 – it appears that the Pountney family found it an uphill task to decide on which pew suited them best.

3 March '... went to hear a concert by Mr Mann's class at Warwick. Lobegesang of Mendlesohn's. Mr Coleridge!!!!!!!!!!!!!!!' Mendelssohn (1809-47) was much admired in Britain, and one of the first performances of his Lobegesang (Hymn of Praise) was in Birmingham in 1840. No more is heard of this Mr Coleridge in the diaries, nor of why Adelaide awarded him so many exclamation marks.

15 April 'Aunt C Mamma L and AMP playing at casino' Ca(s)sino was a popular card game, in which players matched cards in hand with others laid face-up on the table.

23 April '... thence to show Jane the door of the national schools.' The National Society was founded in 1811 to promote education among poor people. Many of their schools, supported in the nineteenth century by charitable donations and events such as school feasts (see 2/9/64), have survived to become the nucleus of the state school system.

21 May 'Jane Miss Burnside Miss Rhodes and I went by the omnibus to Warwick to see the castle.' Visits to stately homes were not very common in Victorian times, as most of them were occupied by their owners, and in no need of tourists. However, the Earl of Warwick welcomed visitors to the state rooms, conservatory and gardens. Visits would have been pre-arranged. The only payment would have been for teas and a tip to the housekeeper. The journey of 3 miles to Warwick by the (horse) omnibus would have taken less than an hour.

The 'Warwick Vase' is a Roman vase, some 4 ft high, from the 2nd century AD. It was found in a lake near Hadrian's Villa in Tivoli. It was acquired by Sir William Hamilton (husband of Emma), heavily restored and given to his nephew the Earl of Warwick. Adelaide's sketch of it in the conservatory is of particular interest, as it has now been replaced by a replica. The original is in Glasgow's Burrell Collection.

7 June 'First day of the Militia band' The Militia was the equivalent of today's Territorial Army. Its part-time soldiers occasionally helped enforce law and order at home, but their prime purpose was to defend the country in time of invasion. Many Militia regiments had their own bands, who would play to the public in bandstands built by the local authorities. Adelaide and her family visited the gardens frequently during the summer to listen to the band, although Adelaide seems to have found it 'quite deafening' (2/7/64).

9 June '...read Nicholas Nickleby to Mysie' Many Victorian families used to read Dickens's novels chapter-by-chapter in monthly periodicals, as they appeared first in as many as twenty instalments in magazines before being sold in book form. Indeed, the first instalments of *Our Mutual Friend* were being published in magazine format throughout 1864/5. Adelaide, however, was clearly reading from the book, as *Nicholas Nickleby* had been published long before, in 1838/9.

10 June '...drove to Kenilworth' From the picture it appears that this visit was to see the castle. It was then, as now, a ruin. Covered in ivy, it suited the Victorian taste for Gothic landscape.

30 June 'Louisa and I took a hospital ticket to Mrs Overton's daughter.' It seems likely that the clothing club contributed also to the cost of some hospital treatment.

30 July 'Overture to Sampa.' Ferdinand Hérold's *Zampa* – Adelaide had a cheerful disregard of the niceties of spelling – was a popular comic opera of the time.

29 August '... to Beck's library' Most towns had a circulating library, such as Beck's, where the middle classes could borrow books for a small rental charge. (See the entries for 24/1/65 and 2/5/65 for the same service in Torquay.) Beck's, printers and stationers in Upper Parade, boasted a stock of 3000 books '*principally* works of fiction'. The annual subscription was 10s. Even after the provision of the public library service, some circulating libraries survived, the last ones closing down in the middle of the twentieth century.

23 September 'Louisa and I went to look for Scott's com. amongst Mr Purton's books.' Presumably this errand was prompted by some urgent request from Mr Purton who needed to consult this reference book. Scott's *Commentary on the Bible* was first published as a weekly magazine from 1788 to 1792. In bound form it became immensely popular in the nineteenth century.

4 October 'Louisa teaching me the linen chest' Louisa was apparently responsible for the care of the family linen. She would have kept the chest locked, and handed out sheets, tablecloths etc to the servants as they were needed. As Louisa was to spend the winter in Torquay looking after her brother, Adelaide now assumed responsibility for the linen, rather as she had to take on the Sunday School teaching when her sisters were away.

6 October 'Rose and I took Rheinardts Terence and other books to Mr Purtons old lodgings.' This hints at a lighter side to Mr Purton. The Roman dramatist Terence was known for his comic verse.

8 October 'The Cotters Saturday night' Some of Adelaide's captions, such as this one, probably echo family jokes. They may have likened cosy evenings on their own to those of cottagers [cotters].

17 October 'Rose and I were made members of the free Library by Mr H Davis.' The Free Libraries were forerunners of the current public library service. The first one in Leamington Spa opened in 1857, with newspapers (see sketch on 22/11/64) and 1000 books. In 1858 it moved to the corner of Bath Street and Church Walk, where a ladies' reading room was opened in 1863. The building survives, much altered. The library has moved.

30 October 'Muller is convicted.' Adelaide makes few comments in her diaries on matters of national concern, but does seem to have taken considerable interest in the fate of criminals. Franz Muller was the first railway murderer in Britain, notorious for throwing his elderly victim from a railway carriage. He fled to the USA, but was immediately arrested by British detectives, who had travelled on a faster ship. Adelaide noted his execution on 14/11/64.

1 November '2nd vol. of haunted hearts' *Haunted Hearts* was by Maria Cummins, then famous as the author of *The Lamplighter*. Adelaide comments that *Haunted Hearts* was a 'clever book'. It may have been, but it has not stood the test of time. It is long out of print.

13 December 'Louisa and I went with Miss Bolt to a meeting for the S.P.G. in the assembly rooms.' The Society for the Propagation of the Gospel in Foreign Parts, established in 1701, was, and is, one the chief missionary societies of the Church of England. No doubt this meeting was to report on its work and raise funds.

1865

10 January 'Mr Richards called to sign Arthur's half pay papers.' Naval officers, when temporarily unfit for service, were retained on half-pay. Arthur seems to have been unwell since his arrival in Leamington in May, although he did return briefly to Devonport.

18 January 'I took the Guardian back to Miss McDougall … posted the usual amount of Standards to Greville' There are very few references to the family reading national newspapers. However, they seem to have sent papers regularly to Greville in Australia. *The Standard* was then a national daily published in London. The Guardian may have been the *Manchester Guardian*, though it was unusual to abbreviate the title.

25 January '… got into a pony fly to come home.' A pony fly was a one-horse carriage, taking fare-paying passengers – the equivalent of today's taxi.

1 February 'Rose and I went into the town & afterwards to the station to regulate our watches.' Before the days of radio, a railway station was one of the few places where one could be sure of finding the right time.

30 March 'Was Pountney thinking of Wilkie. …' Adelaide enjoyed humorously comparing her own sketches to the works of the great painters. (See also 30/6/65 and 8&9/9/65.) Sir David Wilkie (1785-1841) was famous for his anecdotal pictures of village life. He was influenced by the seventeenth-century Dutch and Flemish realists, especially Teniers.

11 April 'We all went to Betts's to buy spring raiment, as the burden of our linseys is greater than we can bear' Linsey was cloth made of linen and wool. It was probably named after Lindsey, in Suffolk, where it was first manufactured.

26 April 'I trimmed Louisa's new Leghorn hat.' A Leghorn was a fine straw hat, tied under the chin with ribbons. Leghorn hats were originally made exclusively from the dried and bleached straw of Italian wheat.

13 June 'The Erl King' The Erlkönig was a ballad from Goethe's ballad-opera *Die Fischerin* (1782). The best known settings were composed by Schubert (1815) and Loewe (1818).

30 June 'We are reminded in the domestic scene of Teniers.' See note on 30/3/65. David Teniers (1610-90) was known for the delicacy of his pictures of peasants.

14 July '... saw many of the mop species of Elms, peculiar to this neighbourhood.' These were probably wych elms, rather than the Cornish elms that were then widespread in Cornwall and Devon.

20 July 'Gladstone turned out of Oxford' This may have been written with glee. If so, it was short lived. Gladstone was not yet Prime Minister, but was the most prominent member of the government and hated by those who objected to his reform of the University. In the 1865 general election, the introduction of postal voting increased the influence of the country clergy, and Gladstone consequently lost his Oxford seat on 17/7/65. However, as multiple nominations were then permissible, he was also nominated for South Lancashire, where he was duly elected on 20/7/65.

25 July 'R read Fortunes of Nigel.' Sir Walter Scott's *Fortunes of Nigel* was first published in 1822.

27 July 'Constance Kent not to be hanged but sent to Australia for life' The three-year-old Francis Kent was murdered in 1860. His step-sister, Constance Kent, confessed to the murder in 1865. In the event, she was not sent to Australia, but kept for twenty years in Millbank prison.

'Dr Pritchard hanged on Thursday.' Dr Pritchard was in fact hanged on Friday 28/7/65, on Glasgow Green, for the murder of his wife, his mother-in-law and possibly a maidservant who died in a fire at his home. It was the last public execution in Scotland.

8 and 9 September 'A Prout' and 'after Snyders ... supposed to be his pupil ...pigs considered very fine' See note on 30/3/65. Samuel Prout (1783-1852) was an English painter known for his water-colours of picturesque buildings. Frans Snyders (1579-1632) was a Flemish painter of animals and still life.

15 September '... the Phaeton unsound on the side where Louisa sat. Mem. not to drive four again if possible.' A phaeton was a light, open, four-wheeled carriage. It was usually drawn by a pair of horses, but the sketch and later references imply that the Pountneys' phaeton was drawn by a single pony.

18 October 'Lord Palmerston died today.' Palmerston died in office as Prime Minister.